THE GREAT MOSQUITO HUNT
AND OTHER ADVENTURES

THE GREAT MOSQUITO HUNT

AND OTHER ADVENTURES

To Susi it's been great knowing you. love from Lizzie

ELIZABETH MANSON-BAHR

Matador
Unit E2 Airfield Business Park,
Harrison Road, Market Harborough,
Leicestershire. LE16 7UL
Tel: 0116 2792299
Email: books@troubador.co.uk
Web: www.troubador.co.uk/matador
Twitter: @matadorbooks

ISBN 978 1 80514 154 9

British Library Cataloguing in Publication Data.
A catalogue record for this book is available from the British Library.

Typeset in 11pt Minion Pro by Troubador Publishing Ltd, Leicester, UK

Matador is an imprint of Troubador Publishing Ltd

In memory of Clinton and Joan

CONTENTS

PROLOGUE

The trunk was old and worn. Judging from the patchwork of shipping labels, its owners had travelled the world. It didn't look much like a school trunk. It was far too big and far too heavy. Inside were letters, photo albums, press cuttings, binoculars, medals, feather pictures, medical texts, a sketchpad and paints. A battered blue stamp album sat on top of a pile of letters tied in string. One dated 1910 from my great-grandfather, Sir Patrick Manson, to his pregnant daughter Edith living in Fiji, advised her how to avoid dysentery: no bad water, no uncooked vegetables or cold food contaminated by flies. He added a postscript.

> *"I wish you had a Chinaman or two about you. They are so clever and resourceful. The Fijian, I fear is very much of a savage still although he has given up on long pig and does not eat the missionary any more."*

The letter would have taken six weeks to reach her. A small missionary boat – the *John Williams*, known by us children as the John Willy – regularly visited the islands delivering missionaries and mail. Patrick Manson had huge respect for the Chinese. It was in China and Hong Kong where he had done his research to discover that insects were vectors of disease. And many were the diseases he identified with his lonely microscope. He became known as 'Mosquito Manson' and founded the London School of Tropical Medicine and the Chinese Medical School of Hong Kong. One of his early students was the first president of China, Sun Yat-sen. Among the letters was a postcard from his daughter Edith to a Fraulein Mendelsohn, apologizing for missing a piano lesson, and condolences for the death of a one-legged man – killed by a buffalo in Tanganyika. More poignant was an obituary from *The British Medical Journal* dated March 22nd 1902.

"On March 15th, a telegraphic message brought the sad news to London that Patrick Thurburn Manson, eldest son of Dr Patrick Manson, had met with a fatal accident shortly after his arrival on Christmas Island. A commission to investigate scientifically and to report upon Beri-Beri was sent to Christmas Island by the London School of Tropical Medicine towards the end of 1901. Dr Durham, one of the members of the commission, left London in November on his way hither and Dr P Thurburn Manson early in January of this year. Dr Manson could only just have reached his destination when the accident happened.

It is sad at any time to see a young life full of promise suddenly cut short, but it is especially sad when the victim, as in this instance, comes forward in the cause of humanity to risk his life so that disease may be checked. Beri-beri is so virulent a disease and so widespread in the Malayan archipelago that it claims thousands of victims yearly and it has ruined many commercial enterprises by the havoc it causes among the labourers engaged in reclaiming land from the forest and cultivating it. It was to investigate the nature of this scourge and its possible prophylaxis that the Commission went out and it was in this noble cause that young Manson lost his life.

This is not the first time he proved his devotion to the cause of science. When his father conceived the notion of testing the transmission of malaria by mosquitos, he wished to do so by allowing mosquitos infected in the Roman Campagna to bite healthy persons in Britain.

His son, Dr P Thurburn Manson, at once offered himself as a subject for experiment and it will be remembered that the experiment was successful and thus Dr P Thurburn Manson became infected with malaria."

Patrick Thurburn Manson was the most promising of Patrick's two sons, a Cambridge Blue with a bright medical future. He did not die of malaria but by the gun in unexplained circumstances. Today we cannot imagine experimenting on our own children. My own father, grandson of Sir Patrick, was part of a group who infected a man with sleeping sickness in the 1960s. The volunteer, a Swiss parasitologist, nearly died.

There were letters from all over the world for Manson was a household name. Those were the days when medical men pursued their experiments alone with their microscopes, guided by their instincts. They had no idea what other researchers might be doing but nothing could quite match the moment of euphoria when the lone scientist knows he has discovered something huge and rushes to tell the world by telegram, hoping that someone else has not got there before him.

Old stamp hinges had left their scars on the pages of the album like chicken pox spots. Headings in a childish hand listed Western Samoa, Ceylon, British Solomon Islands, Cochin and Travancore, New Caledonia, Bechuanaland, Northern and Southern Rhodesia, Fiji, Borneo, New Guinea, Malaya and Tonga. On my 8th birthday my father had given me a first day cover of Pitcairn Island stamps. My father collected only British Empire stamps. "Don't bother with the others," he would say. The Pitcairn Islands now belong to

New Zealand. Forty-eight people live there, walking up the Hill of Difficulty to reach their main town, Adamstown. Their ancestors tried unsuccessfully to escape the pink parts of the globe.

A letter from my grandfather P.H. Bahr, the owner of the trunk, emerged from an envelope at the bottom of the pile. The stamp was Egyptian. The date was April 1919. It was written to my father, aged eight.

"My Dear Clinton, I cannot tell you how much I enjoyed your letter which you wrote to me on March 16th. You really are writing very well now and I very much hope soon to see that you can write a long letter without making a mistake. You must learn to write good letters while you are a young man for you can never learn to do so when you are older.

I am sorry that I cannot get home to see you at school as there has been trouble in Egypt and we are being kept here in order to keep the people in order. Mummy will tell you that I have recently been in Khartoum which is as you know very far away from here in the Sudan and where the people are very black indeed. Please keep well yourself and be ready to welcome grumpy old Daddy whenever this War has finished with him, which let us hope will be soon. I have sent Mummy stamps and postcards for you from Khartoum.

Your loving Daddy."

In 1956 I took possession of the trunk. Now it contained school clothes, all brown skirts, shorts, slippers, lisle tights, elasticated bloomers, a shapeless woollen swimsuit, white shirts, striped ties and had been transported to Winchester, where it sat dejectedly, like us, on a hard stone floor in a suburban villa, which, like the trunk, had seen better days. The house mistress, Mrs Ruston, was brusque.

"We have many colonial girls here," she assured my mother in a disapproving voice. "Elizabeth does look peaky. Her skin is sallow and she is very small for twelve. We will fatten her up. Can she cook or sew?"

"No!" exclaimed my mother who hated both.

"Goodness me. We will have to change that. Our girls are brought up to be useful citizens. We are a very sporty house here. Is Elizabeth good at games? Hillcroft wins all the lacrosse cups."

"Elizabeth is a very good swimmer," my mother retorted proudly.

"There are no cups for swimming," sniffed Mrs Ruston.

She examined my tweed coat – it weighed a ton – brown felt hat and Mary Jane shoes. The clothes swamped my four feet ten frame. Then she turned to my mother in her navy tailored coat with her diamond eagle brooch and French hat. My mother had spent hours deciding how to dress for the occasion. She needed armour to face this day. She was a stranger to English culture. It was as remote to her as if she were living in the Trobriand Islands. Mrs Ruston cast her eye on the trunk.

"It does seem rather large. I hope Elizabeth has not brought too many clothes. We don't encourage our girls to show off."

My mother bristled.

"We have just arrived from Kenya, you know."

It failed to impress. We had already discovered that the inhabitants of England didn't approve of colonials. The trunk itself seemed to diminish too as if its exotic travels did not count for much in this chilling territory. What did seem to count were the rows of silver cups arranged in front of the mirror on the mahogany dresser in the dining room. The gardener appeared and, with my father, manhandled the trunk up three levels to the attic. A long narrow room under the eaves, it was crammed with twelve iron beds, chairs and small chests of drawers. Each bed had a thin mattress, one pillow and two brown blankets. Brown tweed dressing gowns that scratched like hair shirts, hung on pegs at the end of each bed. Even in September it was cold.

"Is there heating for the winter?" asked my mother.

"Heating? Goodness me. Not up here. There is a coal fire in the junior common room."

Mrs Ruston pointed to a small cupboard covered by a curtain.

"Elizabeth will share the cupboard with the next bed."

My mother unpacked my nylon eiderdown and made up the bed.

"Elizabeth suffers from allergies."

Mrs Ruston's mouth took a disapproving curve.

"None of our girls have allergies."

From that moment I became one of her least favourite pupils.

My parents were impatient to leave. They seemed battered. It had started so well.

"You will love it," pronounced my mother. "You can learn the piano. They have grass tennis courts. You are a lucky girl. Your father is spending all this money on you."

I had cried copious tears when the idea was first mooted. I was happy in my colonial school.

"Look, we have to go. Auntie Mary will come and visit you. We'll write."

A girl was assigned to show me the ropes. She stared at me.

"You're not African?"

"I am African."

"Well, you're not black. I only volunteered because I thought you were black. My father says you colonials exploit the Africans."

She gave me a tour of the boarding house. It smelt of damp. The muted colours of the stained-glass windows dominating the stairs matched the uniform. In the common room overlooking the garden, chairs with bulging springs hogged a small coal fire. The more senior you were, the closer you got to the fire and the chilblains. The girl held herself erect. I noticed that she wore a yellow belt. Everyone else had brown.

"It's a posture belt, silly. You have to sit up dead straight for at least three terms." She pointed to the back of the room, furthest from the fire. "You'll be there with the other new girls."

The radio was permitted most evenings. Otherwise everyone read or chatted or mended their socks. Homework was every night before supper. We were all expected to help clear up and tidy and make breakfast in the morning. "We don't have servants here," said Mrs Ruston pointedly. Sundays were for darning and mending in her sitting room.

"It sounds like an orphanage."

"That's not funny," said the girl.

The dining room had five tables seating eight. On the top tables, Mrs Ruston and the matron sat with their favourites. A prefect sat at each of the other tables. Their word was law. Butter was rationed to four ounces per person per week and was kept in individual dishes. There was still some rationing in the 1950s. Some girls ate it all before it went rancid. Others made it last the week. Apples, oranges and bananas cost extra and came in a brown paper bag. Everyone had a half pint of milk in a bottle with a straw, except for the peaky colonials who were given a whole pint with cream swimming on top. And there were the rules: no talking after lights, baths every two days, hair washing once a fortnight, church every Sunday, twice if you were confirmed.

"Some of us are frightfully keen and rush breakfast to go up to school for early practice."

"Practice?"

The girl with the posture belt had still not succumbed to gravity.

"Lacrosse, silly. We have won the house cup for three years running."

Mrs Ruston summed it up at prayers that evening.

"We are a family here."

And that is how I arrived at boarding school in Winchester in September 1956, with a smuggled scarlet dressing gown buried among the grunge clothes, wondering how I would survive the next four years. My brother's experience was even more distressing. At nine he was sent to a prep school in Westgate-on-Sea in Kent where my father and grandfather had gone before him. It might as well have been Siberia, for there was the feeling of being exiled to the outer reaches of the country. It was run by a headmaster who liked beating his pupils' bare bottoms and, when the sun shone, sent them outside to sunbathe naked or enquired rather too frequently whether they 'had been'. This was not considered strange and was thought to be character forming. My brother's strategy for survival was to keep his head down and not complain. He endured and passed his exams. One would ask today why our parents did not choose more suitable schools. They lived far away. One school was much like another. They took the easiest option. My mother had lived in Scotland until the age of twelve before being sent to South Africa as an orphan. She had married into a middle-class English family and was unaware of its tribal customs. Schools were chosen on recommendation or family history. My brother's school was near our grandfather who lived in Kent, the previous owner of my trunk. It was hoped that he might visit from time to time. He had travelled the world for his work as a tropical diseases specialist but he never managed to make it to Westgate-on-Sea. My brother, like so many colonial children, felt abandoned. Both of us had guardians. Mine was very solicitous. My brother's never left his farm. Many children who were educated in the colonies never settled and remained in Africa mode, resigned to uncertain futures in countries that no longer wanted them. So, in that respect we were fortunate and, unlike our forebears, we flew home once a year for the summer holidays and sometimes at Xmas. At that point the summer seemed a long way off. We didn't see our parents for several months.

Mosquito Manson

CHINA 1866–1889

Patrick Manson and family in Amoy (Xiamen), China, 1881

For our great-grandfather, Sir Patrick Manson, in China, it would be nine years before he returned to Scotland. Travel in the mid-19th century was slow and expensive. Patrick was the most famous member of our tribe. I first learnt of him when I was eight. My mother had a habit of dipping into books she would never normally read, like *Manson's Tropical Diseases*. When she thought no one was looking she would open the pages and examine the gruesome illustrations. There would be a sharp intake of breath. One day I looked over her shoulder at a photo of a man lying in a wheelbarrow with an enormously swollen scrotum. She snapped the book shut. "He's got elephantiasis. Your great-grandfather Patrick discovered the causes." I learnt later that Patrick had removed 80lbs of tumour from the patient, who then sued him for loss of earnings. He had used his swollen extremities as a table to sell lemonade and peanuts!

"He was a doctor in China," said my mother, "and a Scot like me. When he was only eleven he shot a wild cat and extracted a tapeworm from its intestines." What she did not say was that he was one of the most important scientists, in that his discoveries saved millions of lives. Later I would learn how key he had been and my brother would follow the family tradition of medicine.

Like many Scots, Patrick found work abroad. In 1866 he joined the Chinese Imperial Maritime Customs Service. This was an organization run by Europeans for the Qing government to collect the maritime trade taxes that had gone unpaid as a result of the Taiping rebellion, and to pay the fines levied by the British and the French during the two opium wars. Its Inspector General, Sir Robert Hart, successfully brought corruption under control and increased the annual revenues. Not only was Sir Robert fluent in Mandarin, but he was also respected for his love of the Confucian classics and by all accounts had two families, one being Chinese. Apart from the collection of taxes, the Chinese Imperial Customs Service managed the harbours and rivers. It mapped and policed the Chinese coast and the Yangtze River. It kept weather charts. It acted as a bank and published Western scientific texts, including Patrick's early research. Patrick was based at a mission hospital first at Takao in Formosa (now Taiwan) where he inspected the ships calling at the port and provided medical care for the sailors. It was a lonely five years for a young man, even one as reserved as Patrick, who was comfortable with his own company. He liked exploring the wilder parts of the island and became friendly with the native inhabitants – the Sheng-fan – wild men, whose language he learnt. He didn't take advantage of the mui-tsai, women who offered sex, companionship and domestic service, preferring to hunt snipe in the marshes. Perhaps he was wary of disease – he saw much of it in his work – or the complications of such relationships. So he concentrated on his work. Most of his research took place in those lonely years in China, although being out of touch with the rest of the world made research difficult. He wrote to a friend.

"I live in an out of the world place, away from libraries, out of the run of what is going on, so I do not know very well the value of my work or if it has been done before or better."

In our age of Google it is hard to imagine Patrick doing such ground-breaking research with a simple lens in the dim light of an oil lamp. At this stage he didn't have a microscope. He relied on clinical skill and meticulous record-keeping. He also managed to build up a lucrative private practice. Within three years he had saved enough money to pay his father the cost of his medical education. He had to save too for a pension since his salary was tied to the fluctuating price of silver and did not cover such benefits. However, private patients were demanding and didn't always pay their bills. One night an American naturalist charged through the door with blood gushing from his nose. An injection of salt and water into the nostril released a leech, which dropped into the kidney dish. "Oh God," screamed the patient, dropping the dish and vanishing like a ghost. Leeches were as common there as verrucas in schoolboys.

In 1871 Patrick moved over the sea to the small island of Amoy (Xiamen), still working for the Maritime Customs Service, but attached to two local mission hospitals. The town, a treaty port, had become one of the most important international ports in China and was the centre of the tea trade. The finest teas came from the Wuyi mountains in the north of the province, an area of sub-tropical hardwood forests that dated back to the last ice age. The ancient walled town of Amoy was squashed onto a boulder-strewn island between wooded hills and the sea. Its deep-water port was long known to traders and pirates. Among its visitors were Marco Polo in the 13th century and Ibn Battuta in the 14th. Bare hills on the edge of town bore testimony to centuries of habitation with graves so tightly packed together that barely a blade of grass showed. Villages and fields of sweet potatoes, rice, groundnuts and vegetables dominated the coastal valleys on the mainland. Bamboo plantations filled the marshes – the province was famous for its bamboo forests, which were more commercially valuable than its celebrated teas. This was home to some of China's richest merchants and also one of its poorest cities, its narrow sunless streets *as crooked as rams' horns*, crammed with beggars and cripples, the dead and the dying. Here and there a pretty curved roof jutted over streets that doubled as latrines, the drain in the middle permanently blocked by sewage and night soil. Scavenging dogs and pigs competed for scraps with hideously deformed people who dragged their swollen extremities through the dirt. These were symptoms of elephantiasis (Patrick had yet to discover its causes).

This living laboratory was a dangerous place to live, endemic for malaria, elephantiasis, typhoid, dengue fever, leprosy, and with regular outbreaks of cholera and plague. Like other Westerners and wealthy Chinese, Patrick chose to live on Gulangyu Island, a short boat ride from Amoy. Now a World Heritage Site visited by millions, then it was a quiet paradise two miles square, a Chinese landscape in miniature with boulders and rocks, mini-canyons, paddy fields of rice and marshes where egrets over-wintered. The sea winds kept disease and mosquitoes at bay. Gulangyu means Drum-Wave Island, so called because of the drumming of the sea on the reefs. It was also the only international settlement on Chinese soil apart from Shanghai. Merchants were beginning to build the villas that are still there today with their domes and spires, tiled eaves, baroque embellishments and classical columns. The few Europeans living there managed to create an active social life with a club, sports facilities and a small theatre. A protestant church, four Chinese temples and one Masonic lodge catered for spiritual nourishment. The Amoy Gazette was printed daily in English. Patrick, however, preferred to hunt snipe and tigers. Perhaps he agreed with the Dutch student who lived on Gulangyu at the time that "*the English women are badly dressed and are terrible flirts. And they do like to sing after supper.*"

In the morning, Patrick saw his private patients at home. After lunch he took a boat to Amoy, rowing between the moored junks with laundry flapping from the masts and the larger ships from America, Britain, Spain, France and Holland. It always pleased him, this rugged beauty of coast and mountains that stretched far into the interior. He knew the backcountry well. It was where he hunted the Chinese golden tiger. He was an excellent shot. There is a family story of him going shooting in Scotland with forty cartridges and returning with thirty-nine pheasants and one unspent cartridge. Hunting expeditions began at dawn with a climb over half-moon bridges onto the stony tracks that led into the interior. An army of Chinese bearers followed carrying sharpened bamboo spikes. The tiger was a worthy opponent. A solitary and silent beast, it camouflaged well in the dense cover of sword grass. You could walk right past and never see it. Because of the large number of tigers the hunts were successful. The poor old tiger hanging limply from poles was displayed in the villages. Everyone wanted a piece, and besides, it was one less tiger to prey on their children. Nothing of the animal was wasted. Gallstones mixed with honey treated abscesses. The eyeballs became pills for convulsions; whiskers were used for toothache. The tail had many uses: its flesh could be ground to make ointment, its bones to ward off evil spirits and there was tiger bone wine. Last but not least was the penis, used as an aphrodisiac. The only tigers left are in a reserve.

But most days were the same, arriving at the port and taking a sedan. A simple chair fixed between two bamboo poles and carried by two to four bearers, it picked its lumbering way to the Baptist Hospital (normally a sedan chair could travel at four miles an hour). The sweat ran down the sunburnt backs of the half-naked coolies as they carried their large European passenger. By now Patrick was inured to the stench of the town. The Chinese disliked water. They believed that the upper body, the Yang, was the heavenly part, whereas the lower, the Ying, was connected to the earth. Washing risked contaminating the heavenly Yang with the earthier Ying. As he approached the Baptist Hospital the streets opened up. Women tottered on their bound feet. A woman without bound feet was not considered good marriage material. Those who had suffered the pain of binding – and Patrick would have seen their feet as he treated them – would have learnt not to complain. 'Rise, run (difficult on their 'golden lilies'), work, eat little, spend little, be silent, obey, bear' were the rules that governed their lives. He had huge respect for the ordinary Chinese, for their resourcefulness, their hardiness, their cunning and their cheerfulness in the face of such adversity, despite the fact that the inhabitants of Fujian province, including Amoy, were reputed to be the rudest people in China.

Patrick doubled as surgeon and physician. He said of himself that he was 'an indifferent surgeon but a good carpenter'. He took risks; he had no choice. He designed his own tools and had them made up by a Chinese metal worker. One such was Manson's trocar and cannula for draining liver abscess (a death sentence then) without the need for an operation. In 1872 he removed one ton of blubber and impressive amounts of blood from 237 patients, including the man who arrived wheeling his scrotum in a wheelbarrow. All without antibiotics or blood transfusions and with only two deaths despite the tremor in his hand. This was in part due to a special table that Patrick designed – he liked gadgets. It had a board on which the patient lay, which could be tipped, using gravity to drain the excess blood from the tumour. During his long, lonely nights with his microscope, Patrick had noticed a tiny worm in the blood of so many of his patients that he felt sure there was some connection between those worms and elephantiasis. He could not, however, work out why the worms were not always present in the blood. This discovery came later and was triggered by the researches of an army surgeon in India. However, Patrick had no one with whom to discuss this. When he wrote to the British Museum for information on mosquitoes, they sent him a book on cockroaches! Both Western and Chinese medicine were impotent in the face of tropical disease. The constant hunt for parasites nearly led Patrick to an early death. He had bought a corpse he knew harboured parasites. It had been left as promised, in a dimly lit room in a temperature of 40°C. Sweating heavily and trying to ignore the stench, he prepared to examine the corpse with his brother who had joined him in Amoy, when they heard shouting, "Death to the foreign devils." They only just escaped. The widow disappeared with her 200 silver dollars paid in advance.

Patrick was now twenty-eight and beginning to suffer from the gout that would trouble him all his life. This didn't stop him working all hours. He had always been passionate about medical education and set up classes for local Chinese. These became popular. But the Baptist Hospital thought this a distraction from their main purpose, to spread the Christian message, so Patrick moved to the Seamen's Hospital in the native quarter, where he set up consulting rooms, a small hospital and a cash dispensary. This didn't go down well with the mission hospital, although it generated much-needed income for Patrick. He had seen how the Chinese doctors worked in the open, so his operating room had large windows facing the street. This allowed the nervous relatives to press their faces to the glass to check that the surgeon wasn't murdering his patients. It worked. Although the Chinese were suspicious of Western doctors – they were thought to eat Chinese babies and use their hearts for potions – news of his success spread. Soon wealthy Chinese attended his clinics, the wily mandarins sending their servants to test the waters before submitting themselves. Patrick's private list and income grew with his reputation. He built up a successful private practice (he did well in obstetrics), which served both Chinese and European patients, including the British Consul. In 1875 he took a year's leave (his brother David stood in for him) and returned to England. He had been away for nine years. At thirty-one, he was a man in need of a wife.

On arrival he went first to his home in the small granite town of Oldmeldrum in Aberdeenshire. It sits on a ridge among the fertile flat lands north of Aberdeen and looks westward towards the Cairngorms and Bennachie Hill. The Mansons were a prominent family of farmers and businessmen, descendants of Norwegian pirates, as Patrick described them. In 1797 they had started an illegal distillery, Glen Garioch, now part of the Suntory Group. Patrick's father was a local laird and bank manager, and his formidable mother, Elizabeth Livingstone Blaikie, came from an Aberdeen family who owned an iron foundry. They had nine children, many of them scattered to the winds, one dying of yellow fever in Havana.

Patrick Manson's birthplace in Oldmeldrum, Aberdeenshire

Patrick's grandfather, Patrick Blaikie, after whom he was named, was a naval surgeon whose ship had taken Napoleon to exile on Elba. He found the emperor charming and grateful for the protection of the Royal Navy, fearing that the French would assassinate him. It must have been a pleasant change for Patrick in the gentle landscapes of home with its soft grey light and low scudding clouds. These were the spaces of his childhood where he used to run wild exploring the natural world that surrounded him. He caught up with his relatives. He fished. He hunted rabbits and partridge and no doubt ruminated on the causes of tropical diseases, which were jumbled in his mind like the pieces of a jigsaw. Perhaps he smiled at the thought that he had proved his teachers wrong – dismissed as an unpromising pupil – and thankful for his prodigious memory (he could recite the sermons in church at the age of five). He had always loved the natural world. This passion had led him to study medicine after developing curvature of the spine and partial paresis of his right arm when working in his mother's family's foundry, leaving him with a tremor for the rest of his life.

After three months at home, Patrick returned to London to take a course in ophthalmology at Moorfields. Then he spent his time in the British Library, where in March 1875 he made a major discovery in the writings of Timothy Lewis, a surgeon in the Indian Army Medical Service, who had reported the discovery of a tiny nematode worm in human blood, which he named Filaria sanguinis hominis. He recognized that these tiny worms represented the embryonic stage of some larger fully developed creatures in the human body. Patrick would have known nothing of this in China. This must have been a eureka moment, for it confirmed what he had felt for some time but could not yet fit together. While in London he was invited to a lunch party given by a Colonel Thurburn in Norwood. There he met Henrietta Isabella Thurburn. She was bright, beautiful and spoke three languages. Years of living alone had made him self-reliant but a man could not live alone forever in a foreign country with only his microscope for company. They married in Campden Hill in 1875. He was thirty-one, she eighteen. They left for China, taking with them a new compound microscope. A new wife and a new microscope, not bad going for a holiday.

At Gulangyu Island, Henrietta Isabella and Patrick disembarked, taking care not to slip on the granite slabs of the causeway where their boat had landed among the fishing junks clogging the harbour. On the rock towering above them, the ghost of Koxinga looked down. A local hero and Ming loyalist, he had resisted the Qing conquest of China and defeated the Dutch in Taiwan. Coolies took the couple and their trunks to their new home. As they travelled in the dusk, did they see the ghosts of the 550 British soldiers and three ships left on the island after the Battle of Amoy in 1841 during the First Opium War? Despite the heat the British had fought in full uniform. What had killed them, however, was disease. It was said that their ghosts scrambled restlessly over the island and only Chinese gongs and drums could drive away their spirits.

Colonial villas on Gulangyu Island, Amoy (Xiamen), China
John Holmes/Alamy stock photo

There were no spirits in Patrick's new home, a large colonial villa with wide verandahs on both floors to catch the breeze. The house stood among boulders on a rocky hill shared with the newly built villas of the Chinese merchants. The population had grown since Patrick first moved there. Now there were 251 foreigners, including British, German, American, Portuguese, Spanish, Japanese, and Danish, and 2,835 Chinese residents. Servants greeted them, an amah for the children, a houseboy, cook, girl to clean, a boy jack-of-all trades and a sampan man to ferry them across to Amoy. Social life was busy too. The club was open and running. You could get ice and soda water and milk that wasn't watered down. The Danish Telegraph Company had moved in and there was a proper customs house.

It was all very different, however, from Buenos Aires, where Henrietta Isabella had spent her early years in a bubble of British culture, in leafy suburbs with names like Banfield and Temperley, in houses that looked like those in Surrey. She had attended English schools and Scottish churches and played tennis at the club. She called England home. Many British had come to Argentina in the 19th century as investors and landowners to develop the pampas for beef and wool and set up meat-packing and refrigeration facilities. Others went as engineers to build the railways. Some came as missionaries and whalers. Henrietta Isabella's brother, Robert, worked for the Bank of London and South America, which became known in popular parlance as 'Thurburn's Bank'. Her father, James Ptolemy Thurburn, had come to Buenos Aires as a captain in the Royal Navy. Half Scottish, half French, born in Egypt, he married a Scottish girl in Buenos Aires. He went wherever the Navy sent him, but every ten years the family returned to England, renting houses in London, Scotland, Lincolnshire and eventually ending up in Norwood in London.

Soon after the newlyweds' arrival, a devastating cholera outbreak struck Amoy. The dead and the dying piled up in the streets and there was little room left in the cemeteries on the hill. Patrick dispensed anti-diarrhoea medicines free of charge at his dispensary, aided by the local mandarins. But medicine was not enough. Devil-scaring ceremonies were required to pacify the mob. When normal life resumed, there was the house to be made comfortable with bamboo blinds, potted plants and tiger skins on the wooden floors. In the late afternoon Patrick and Henrietta Isabella strolled on the island paths, listening to the sea drumming on the rocks, admiring the glossy leaves and spreading roots of the banyan trees and the stately betel nut palms whose dried red nuts were sold in the markets. Betel nut was considered a scourge; it involved a lot of spitting, which left blood-red stains all over the island. They inspected the ancient inscriptions and climbed up to Sunlight Rock to join Koxinga on his eternal watch over the sea. They paddled on the small sandy beach and admired the colourful temples with their curved tiled roofs. There was a new arrival on the way and there was loss too. Their first son Thurburn was born in 1878 and Patrick's brother David died of sunstroke in Foochow just up the coast in the same year. But the muse still beckoned and there was that microscope to put to use. Patrick returned to his monastic existence, but not quite, for children appeared regularly. Inspired by the writings of Timothy Lewis that he had discovered in the British Museum, he wanted to solve the riddle of the tiny embryo worm he had spotted in the blood of his patients. He had discovered that they were even more common in South China than India. With his new microscope he could see the worms in greater detail. He pursued his worms with the patience of the hunter, observing their struggle to escape their transparent sheaths to the next stage of development. He put some blood on a slide and stained it. The embryo continued to wriggle like a competitor in a sack race. Might it be a question of temperature? He tried ice to cool down the slide. The reaction was instant. The sheath ruptured; the little worm slithered out and swam around in the blood like an eel. This indicated a connection with a cold-blooded creature in its life cycle. It was a mystery too that the embryo-worms seemed to disappear from the blood during the day. Where did they go? Then fate played its hand. "*It is the discrepancy which teaches you, if you would learn,*" Patrick wrote in his diary. He now had several assistants he had trained to take blood. Of the most able, one worked at night, having to care for a disabled mother during the day; the other turned up at 8am to do the day shift. Patrick found that the daily worker had few, if any, filariae in his blood compared to the boy who worked nights. He repeated the experiment on his gardener Hin Lo, who was already infected with the parasite, isolating him in a room and taking his blood every three hours day and night for fourteen days. The results confirmed his findings that the worm appeared only at night in the human body and that it escaped its sheath and freed itself outside the blood at a lower temperature on its journey to find a new host. Patrick dismissed fleas, bugs, lice as hosts – they were found all over the world in places where there was no filariasis. He settled on the most common insect in Amoy, the small brown mosquito. Here again Hin Lo, the gardener, obliged. There is a painting by Ernest Board in the Wellcome Collection of Hin Lo lying on his bench in his specially built 'mosquito house,' dwarfed by an outsized Patrick in his white tropical suit. To the right of the painting is a tiny Chinese assistant holding out a tray with glass phials. The door to the house was fitted with a spring hinge, which opened inwards, and the hut was covered with mosquito-proof gauze. Each night a light was placed beside Hin Lo and the door left open for half an hour. By morning the gauze was thick with mosquitoes gorged with his blood. Patrick stupefied them with tobacco smoke and put them into phials of water. Many different kinds of mosquitoes were trapped on the gauze but only the common brown mosquito of Amoy carried the worm. He noticed that after feeding (two and a half minutes), the mosquitoes became too heavy to fly and attached themselves to something solid near stagnant water where they digested the blood and waited to lay their mature eggs. As the eggs emerged, floating on the surface of the water (they would hatch into new mosquitoes within ten days), Patrick became emotional. He found the eggs beautiful, comparing them to Etruscan vases. He was tired. His gout was troubling him and his research seemed endless. Night after night in humid heat, the sweat running down his face, he dissected his mosquitoes with a pen nib, finding them more complex than he had ever imagined. He grew to admire these almost invisible creatures in their struggle for life, fulfilling the duty of all living beings to survive and breed.

> *"I shall not easily forget the first mosquito I dissected. I tore off its abdomen and succeeded in expressing the blood the stomach contained. Placing this under the microscope, I was gratified to find that so far from killing the filariae, the digestive juices of the mosquito seemed to have stimulated it to fresh activity."*

He discovered that the embryos ended up in the thoracic muscles of the female mosquito – he called her the nurse – where they increased in size and developed a mouth and other organs. But how the worms moved from there to transmission to humans wasn't discovered until 1900 when it was found that they migrated from the thoracic muscles to the mosquito's proboscis and were injected into a new host in the mosquito's saliva. They then travelled to the lymph glands where they grew into adults, mating and releasing millions of micro worms into the blood, causing the symptoms of lymphatic filariasis. This was ground-breaking research in 1877. It was the clue to solving the puzzle of malaria and other insect-borne diseases. The very idea that insects could be vectors of disease was thought absurd. Little was known of mosquitoes, let alone the possibility that they might be agents of disease. Patrick continued to dissect all manner of creatures: dogs, crows, magpies and mynah birds – many of which were found to have filariae in their blood. A second attempt to examine a corpse had proved more successful than the first. He had discovered a mass of worms, 200 or so, in the dead man's stomach and identified them as tapeworms. It was the first time they had been discovered in humans. Still, it was risky to buy corpses and there was no need to run the gauntlet of a murderous mob. So he stuck to animals and birds until his Chinese friends informed him that, as everyone knew, the soul of a Chinese emperor had entered a magpie. What if he happened to kill that particular bird?

His research was published in the *Imperial Maritime Customs Report* in 1877 and then in the *Journal of the Linnean Society* in London in 1878. The paper was read out but the fellows were not impressed. One old member stood up: "Good God, are we expected to believe that these filariae are provided with watches so they know when to retire and when to get up?" This was followed by shrieks of laughter. Another Fellow suggested the paper was either the work of genius or, more likely, the emanations of a drunken Scots doctor in far-off China, where everyone knew they imbibed far too much whisky. None of this deterred Patrick. He had found the key to the terrible diseases he had seen in China and he had done it alone in distant Amoy. When my grandmother Edith was born in 1879 she narrowly escaped being christened Filaria. Another chance discovery added to the collection. An important mandarin consulted Patrick about a boil on his face. He arrived coughing and some of his blood-stained sputum landed on the carpet. Patrick knelt on the floor and scraped up the spit. Under the microscope he found yellow oval eggs, possibly belonging to a worm. As he explained:

"I was not looking for a parasite when I found these eggs, for a man may search for a shilling and find a sovereign. The important thing is to search."

The mandarin returned and repeated the performance into jars of water. After two weeks, tiny embryos escaped from the eggs and swam around like fish searching for a host. Patrick thought of a water-based host. Snails were as common as spitting. He identified these embryos as lung-flukes that passed from man to man through freshwater snails in the water, but this remained unproven until 1916. Many creatures apart from humans suffer from liver fluke in South Asia, many from eating raw freshwater crabs. It was another piece in the jigsaw and led the way to the conquest of malaria, sleeping sickness and bilharzia. Patrick used a fishing metaphor for his research.

> *"I came to London principally with the view to rub myself up in medicine and surgery. But it was like fishing in a big lake for the two or three fish the big lake might or might not hold. I did not know where the particular fish I wanted lay, and I found no one to tell me where they lay or how to set about hooking them, and I finally landed at the Reading Room of the British Museum. Dreary enough and profitless enough was the fishing there, as you can imagine."*

But he did hook one good fish in Timothy Lewis's report on Filaria sanguinis hominis.

In 1882 it was time for another holiday and the journey home. In 1866, pre-Suez, Patrick would have travelled to China in an iron-clad clipper powered by coal and wind. The journey would have taken over three months, calling at many ports to refuel. That same year sixteen British and American clippers were racing back in the opposite direction, competing for the Great Tea Race. The result was 26,000 kilometres in ninety-nine days. When the Suez Canal was completed in 1869 it took twelve days off the journey. Now it was so much quicker to travel. P&O ran a steam ship service from China via Calcutta. The family, there were three children now, spent six months at Littlewood on the banks of the Don in Patrick's native Aberdeenshire among pine forests and heather-covered hills with partridges and pheasants and rivers brimming with salmon and trout. This must have been a happy time relaxing in the panelled rooms with their tapestries and sporting prints. There had been a new arrival, Alexander, born at Littlewood. In the evening Patrick would have a wee dram or two and drop off in front of a log fire. The climate was a respite and the midges in summer, although annoying, were not vectors of disease. Although Amoy was a first-rate place for clinical experience and research, it was not the best place to bring up a family. There were schools to be considered and financial considerations to be made. Patrick needed a larger income. He had a growing family to provide for and there was always the problem of a pension. Hong Kong was just the place. It was where people went to make money. It was not so out of the way and he would be more in the swing of things, although he would have less time for research. After his peaceful sojourn on the banks of the Don, he returned to Amoy, packed up and moved further down the coast to the Crown colony of Hong Kong in 1883 to set up in private practice. Despite its reputation as a white man's graveyard, Hong Kong offered a more attractive way of life for the growing family and a chance for Patrick to prosper. Patrick's arrival would have been noted under 'New Arrivals' in *The China Mail*. He set up his practice treating Chinese and European patients. But even in Hong Kong it wasn't easy to establish a new practice since the colony was crawling with doctors. He persevered with long days, some ten to twelve hours divided between the practice and the Alice Memorial Hospital where he operated. The Hospital was founded by Patrick's friend Sir Ho Kai, a fellow alumnus of Aberdeen Medical School, in memory of his young wife Alice who died of typhoid. The family home in The Albany, a new development set among trees, was close to the tennis club, which opened in 1883 after a petition from nineteen ladies, including the governor's wife, to set up a ladies' recreation ground. They were a determined group. Louisa Coxon drove her own pony cart in the annual races in Happy Valley; Mrs William Marsh, the acting governor's wife, entertained at her home Mountain Lodge on top of the peak. There was Mabel Cantlie, the wife of Patrick's new partner Dr James Cantlie, another graduate of Aberdeen, and Amelia Dare, whose mother had been kidnapped by pirates off the coast of Singapore in 1841 and escaped to tell the tale. The tennis club occupied a large site surrounded by trees and with wide views of the bay. In February 1884, when the first four tennis courts were ready, the club held its opening day. The cold and blustery weather did not stop play. In between games the ladies sat in wicker chairs in their long-sleeved shirts and ankle-length skirts, drinking tea. Henrietta Isabella proved a keen member, sharing the silver trophy for mixed doubles in 1887 with twenty-three-year-old George Potts. The ladies, not to be outdone by the men, also fielded a cricket team.

The Albany on Garden Road overlooked the Botanical Gardens and was home to the superintendent of the gardens, who lived in Gardener House. Other houses had nostalgic names like Blue Bungalow and Devonia. It also had a bird's-eye view of the Albany Filter Beds, which looked like bleached rice paddies carved into the contours of the hill. These beds cleaned the water by filtering it through sand and removing bacteria through the sticky residue on its surface. They were popular excursion venues. You could walk down Bowen Road and over the water conduits down Cotton Tree Drive to the Albany Nullah taking advantage of the shaded streets. In 1889, these filter beds flooded, sending landslides down onto the city below. Later, when the peak tram was in operation, the family moved to a large bungalow on the peak 1,500 feet above the city, where it was cooler and windier, with a view over the harbour and its islands. Before the tram, travellers were carried up and down the hill by coolies. You had to be rich to live there. Many large companies were arriving. There was the Taikoo Sugar Refining Company, the largest sugar refinery east of Suez. Swire started with a textile business and Lane Crawford opened a department store and bakery. Patrick was doing well. My grandmother Edith remembered streams of gold coins falling from his pockets after a day's work. She remembered too the menagerie of animals they kept: monkeys, birds and a hunting dog. Patrick's research paid the price for this financial bounty. The family shared this eyrie with many notable people, including E R Belios, the chairman of the Hong Kong Shanghai Bank, an Indian-born Jew who commuted to the centre of town on a camel. Other neighbours included Sir Paul Chater, an

Armenian born in Calcutta and more British than the British, whose obsession was cricket. The Jardine family nearby posted watchmen at their lookout who galloped down on ponies to inform head office when a company boat was approaching.

For Henrietta Isabella, Hong Kong offered a more European life with hotels, museums, libraries and clubs. Every sport was catered for. The grandest club was the Hong Kong Club on Queen's Road, which was a hangout for the Taipans. There was the Hong Kong Jockey Club, the Happy Valley racecourse, the Victoria Recreation Club. Societies such as the St Andrews Society held its Burns Supper as well as grand balls for St Andrews Day and Hogmanay. A lively amateur dramatic society laid on plays. There was no need for hissing oil lamps. This city was lit with gas. There were friends and schools for the children. The dark side to life was disease. The graveyards in Happy Valley showed that the dead were mainly young, many of them soldiers from the garrison and children under five, including Patrick and Henrietta's son Alexander Livingstone. The large military garrison of Indian and English soldiers stationed on the island lost 3% of their men annually to malaria. Patrick thought that malaria resulted from the emanations from swamps harbouring bacilli. He did many experiments, some on himself, but without results. Had he heard of the Frenchman Alphonse Laveran's observation of the malarial parasite in blood taken from patients in Algeria in 1880, he might have reached a different conclusion. But as he himself said, he was far away from learned society. Laveran suggested that mosquitoes were vectors for malaria. Like Manson, Laveran was mocked for this hypothesis, but was recognized with a Nobel Prize in 1907.

For the Chinese inhabitants in the district of Taipingshan, life was altogether more basic. The population increased constantly with migrants pouring in from China. They lived in crowded conditions in streets flooded by blocked drains (the British Colonial

Government refused to renew the drains), sharing their homes with a variety of animals. Pigs lived under the beds and in the kitchens and every floor sported some kind of animal whose urine and faeces dropped through the uneven floorboards to the rooms below. One colonial doctor found a patient dying of smallpox with a joint of meat hanging above his bed. Lavatories, holes in the kitchens, were blocked with sewage. All these health hazards contributed to the regular epidemics that broke out until a fire in 1878 cleared many of the slums. There was a problem with water as the population grew. Some homes had wells contaminated by sewage. Otherwise the inhabitants collected water from the mountain streams, which dried up in the winter. In 1864 the Pokfulam reservoir built in the New Territories soon proved inadequate. Not until the 1970s were huge reservoirs built in the New Territories and a water pipeline brought from mainland China. This was all a long way from Hong Kong's beginnings as a small fishing village on one of the best natural harbours in the world. It was one of 260 islands mostly unpopulated or inhabited by pirates like Madame Ching who commanded over 300 junks and 20,000 pirates and terrorized the south coast, including Amoy and Hong Kong, in the 19th century. No wonder Lord Palmerston wasn't impressed when Captain Elliot seized Hong Kong in 1841. Why the hell had he bothered with a small barren island instead of the more strategic islands further north? Although Patrick had seen terrible poverty in Amoy, Hong Kong was after all a British Crown Colony. Not only did the Chinese children suffer illnesses, many of the garrison children died. Like most Europeans, Patrick considered milk an essential part of a healthy diet. Milk then was imported from native buffaloes and a few sickly cows – some families kept their own but the milk soured in the heat. One entrepreneur kept cows in his cellar in artificial light. Brought in as calves, there was only one way out. The Chinese didn't share the English love of all things dairy. They considered consumers of meat and dairy uncivilized, although they ate almost every animal, including dogs. The cow was unknown in China until the 19th century.

Patrick came up with an enterprising proposal, to set up a proper hygienic dairy with cows from Australia and America. He enlisted the help of his partner James Cantlie who, as the son of a farmer, was well versed in the keeping of cattle. After scouring the countryside, they settled on Pokfulam near the reservoir, four miles from the city centre. Although it was steep and rocky, it had cool breezes, good drainage and, more importantly, a stream. Cows are thirsty creatures who drink ten gallons of water per day. The land was cleared and sown with guinea grass from Australia. Cow huts were built and fodder storage huts with indoor paddocks so the cows could stay inside during the hot summers. The octagonal cow huts were based on huts in the American west. Poisonous snakes were a problem. In summer the cows fed on grass and in winter rice straw with wheat bran and groundnuts. This had to be imported and carried 350ft uphill from the harbour. Frequent typhoons sometimes prevented the unloading of the boats. Despite these careful preparations, the cows didn't appreciate the climate and the bulls refused to perform in the heat. Patrick expanded into ice production in underground cellars to preserve the milk – giving the company the cumbersome name of Dairy Farm Ice and Cold Storage Co. Ltd. After he left Hong Kong most of the herd were killed by rinderpest. A Chinese cowman managed to save what remained by moving the cows inland. The company still exists as the Dairy Farm Company Ltd, part of Jardine Matheson, while the cow sheds have been turned into an arts centre.

Patrick's patients, a mixture of Europeans and Chinese, doubled in two years. But sometimes the Chinese healers proved more knowledgeable than him. One patient who lived on the peak suffered from acute pernicious anaemia, which Patrick had been unable to cure. When he met her again, she showed no signs of sickness.

"Oh," she said. "I got tired of you Scots doctors, so I consulted a Chinese joss doctor. He gave me some pills. I have no idea what they were."

They were dried crows' liver, used by the Chinese for centuries.

Some mandarins, however, preferred Western doctors. Just before Christmas 1887 a summons came to sail north to Tientsin (now Tianjin) to attend the great Chinese statesman Li Hung-chang, who had cancer of the tongue. Tientsin was 1,157 nautical miles north by sea. Patrick was so ill with gout that he had to be carried on board the ship. No doubt Henrietta Isabella tried to stop him going. She might reasonably have asked why the mandarin hadn't chosen one of the local doctors at the hospital he had funded in Tientsin. It was a long arduous trip in winter, in capricious weather.

Li Hung-chang, Marquis Suyi of the Qing Empire
CPA Media Pte Ltd/Alamy stock photo

The man might die anyway and Patrick was in poor health. But the aristocratic Li Hung-chang was an intriguing and important patient. He was everyone's idea of a scholarly mandarin with perfect cheekbones, narrow Manchu eyes and a long wispy moustache.

As Viceroy of Zhili (now Hebei) he helped shape the Qing empire's foreign policy. A general in the Qing army, he was also a diplomat and advisor to the dowager empress, counsellor to the emperor and tutor to the crown prince. He realized that China had to modernize but this proved an uphill struggle in the deeply conservative society of 19th-century China. Patrick's journey took him north along the coast past Amoy and Gulangyu, through the heaving seas off the straits of Formosa, past Shanghai and up into the Gulf of Bohai on the Yellow Sea. So much sediment ran from the confluence of the rivers there that larger vessels had to moor off shore. It was snowing as Patrick was helped into the small boat that took him into harbour where the viceroy's servants waited with a silk-lined palanquin to transfer him to the old walled city of Tientsin. It was a slow journey through empty streets, the only sound the crunch of snow underfoot. He pulled his coat tightly round him – the winds of northern China were bitter. At last the carriage stopped in front of gates lit by red lanterns. A servant led Patrick through a courtyard, past pots emptied of their summer chrysanthemums, and into a large hall with wooden columns. Gold-lettered scrolls hung on the walls and the lacquered chests boasted exquisite porcelain vases. The sixty-four-year-old mandarin huddled in his fur cape next to a brazier. He had difficulty speaking, for his throat was painful and swollen. It wasn't cancer. It was an abscess. Once it was lanced, Li Hung-chang was soon restored to health. He wrote to Patrick.

"On account of a recent slight malady at the root of my tongue I have had the honour to receive your visit from afar. My thanks I am unable to express, and your treatment has

already resulted in a complete cure. Calm then, your anxiety on my account. I send you enclosed a photograph which may perhaps serve you as a reminder of the sincerity of our good feelings toward one another and I hope you will accept it. This is the object of my letter and I take this opportunity of wishing you an elegant time. My card is enclosed. Kuang Hsii, 13th year, 10th moon and 20th day."

There was no offer of a fee but the viceroy agreed to become patron of the new medical school in Hong Kong. This new lease of life enabled Li Hung-chang to travel widely. In 1896 Queen Victoria presented him with the medal of a Knight Grand Cross of the Royal Victorian Order, which he wore pinned onto his silk jacket. He toured the country by train – he wanted to introduce trains to China – and travelled on a boat across Lake Windermere. He attended the coronation of Nicholas II of Russia as representative of the Qing government and visited America and Canada. In Europe he met the wily Bismarck. A French newspaper labelled him 'the yellow Bismarck'. When the *New York Times* asked whether he favoured the introduction of European- or American-style newspapers into China, his reply was prescient.

"There are newspapers in China but the Chinese editors, unfortunately, do not tell the truth. They do not, as your papers, 'tell the truth, whole truth and nothing but the truth'. The editors in China are great economizers of the truth; they tell only part of it. They do not have, therefore, the great circulations that your papers have. Because of this economy of the truth, our papers fail in the mission of a great press, to be one of the means of civilization."

Li-Hung-chang became a patron of the Hong Kong College of Medicine. He died aged 78 in 1901, still a patron.

Patronage of his new college by someone as prestigious as Li Hung-chang was a coup for Patrick. In 1886 he and his colleagues had set up the Hong Kong Medical Society, which evolved into the College of Medicine backed by his friend Sir Ho Kai's money and with himself as its first dean. One of their first pupils was Sun Yat-sen, the first president of modern China. An old Chinese saying echoed Patrick's feelings.

The top physician heals a nation
The middle physician heals patients
The mediocre physician heals disease.

Patrick was now forty-two. He still worked ten to twelve hours a day in the heat, operating as well. This left him little time for research or for his growing family. His oldest son Thurburn was eleven and Edith ten and there were four others, younger. His gout sapped his energy. He had visions of a country estate where he could hunt and fish and perhaps do the odd bit of research. He could afford it. He had done well in Hong Kong. Still it must have been a wrench to leave his new medical school and the dairy farm and his friends, including Dr Ho Kai and James Cantlie. He had come to China twenty-three years ago and seen only dirt and poverty, seeing laziness where there was disease. His admiration of the Chinese had grown. He saw in his students armies of doctors bringing the terrible diseases of Southern China under control. His colleagues and students presented him with an engraved silver cup on a base of entwined lotus stems. In 1889 the family packed up the house and went home. His plans to buy a small estate in Scotland were dashed by the unexpected depreciation in the Chinese dollar. Now the family's income was suddenly reduced. Fate had played its hand. Had Patrick retired, there might never have been a London School of Tropical Medicine and perhaps his collaboration with Ronald Ross, to prove mosquitoes as carriers of malaria, might not have happened. Now he had to start all over again at the age of forty-six and in poor health. It was back to the urban life in London and a five-storey town house in Queen Anne Street. At first it was hard going. Patrick had no professional network in London, despite having been appointed Medical Advisor to the Colonial Office in 1897 when he was in Hong Kong. In the medical fraternity, alumni from Scottish medical schools were not considered equal to those from Oxford, Cambridge or London, and Scottish and Irish doctors filled the medical posts in the Empire. Whereas Patrick was well known in Hong Kong, here few people had heard of him. Ironically although he was settled in the Imperial hub of London with its libraries and societies, there was less opportunity for research than in China. So he took the unusual step of setting up his own lab on the fifth floor. 'The Muck Room' he called it. No one, not even family, was allowed in without his permission. But if you were important enough or could boast of harbouring interesting parasites you were welcomed. Inside was orderly disorder. Dishes, microscope slides, glass bottles of fluids and gadgets, pieces of string, odd bits of wire, anything that might be useful. There were live inhabitants too, caged birds, java sparrows, canaries, guinea pigs and rats whose blood he examined for parasites. There were pets: Isabella Henrietta's monkey and a bad-tempered parrot called Polly who spoke broad Doric. There was also at one time a pet alligator whose eggs were eaten for breakfast. Instead of Amazon deliveries, there were deliveries of live bottled mosquitoes. The old habits continued with long working days and nights. Sometimes Patrick never went to bed despite his daughters climbing up to the Muck Room to plead with him to get some sleep. But sleep eluded him and working took his mind off the ever-present gout. Now the night sounds were urban. Patrick was ingenious too in his search for unusual parasites. In one case a troupe of Dahomey acrobats were performing in the Crystal Palace. Patrick rushed over there, took their blood and found the expected parasites. But this did not bring in work. So the first thing he did

Patrick Manson in his consulting room in London

was to contact the missionary societies; they at least knew who he was. He corresponded too with doctors who sent him blood slides and other specimens from Central Africa. He felt certain that many different forms of blood parasites existed. So it was no surprise to find new filariae in the blood of Congolese patients sent to London suffering from 'negro lethargy' – the name then for sleeping sickness. Private patients were examined in Patrick's fashionably cluttered sitting room with its silver-framed photos and bits and pieces from China, Cantonese cider jugs, ivory carvings and lamps made from porcelain vases. Among the paintings on the walls were newspaper cartoons of himself.

Between his consulting room and the Muck Room, there were four floors, with the servants' bedrooms and a nursery on the fourth, family bedrooms on the third floor, other bedrooms and a drawing room on the second, and on the first a grand parlour and Patrick's consulting room. The kitchens and cellars were in the basement.

After Patrick obtained his membership of the Royal College of Physicians, he became physician to the Seamen's Hospital in Greenwich on the ship, *Dreadnought*. Six years later he moved to the new hospital at the Victoria and Albert Docks. Here he could further his research. Now he had a huge correspondence with doctors around the world. His daughters became his secretaries – Edith, my grandmother, wrote up his research notes and his letters. Henrietta Isabella was his translator. He also researched bilharzia, a parasitic disease that was prevalent in ancient Egypt, and continued his research into the malarial parasite. 51 Queen Anne Street was a busy home with people coming and going, not only visitors from all over the world, but also members of the committees at the London School of Tropical Medicine who met regularly in the downstairs parlour.

In 1896 a former pupil turned up unexpectedly. Sun Yat-sen, Patrick's brilliant student at the Hong Kong School of Medicine, had practised as a doctor but soon gravitated to politics. Many of the young medical students in Hong Kong wanted to modernize their country and bring about the collapse of the conservative Qing government. Sun was forced to flee and turned up in Queen Anne Street. During dinner, to which other Hong Kong friends had been invited, Patrick warned him to avoid the Chinese legation. But Sun either forgot or wanted to use any incident to bring the world's attention to his cause. Whatever, he was lured through the doors of the legation. Sun managed to hide a note in a coal scuttle, which reached Patrick. First attempts to elicit help from officials failed. So Patrick and his friend James Cantlie spent all night on guard outside the Chinese legation, making sure that Sun was not removed to a watery death. In the morning Patrick went straight to Lord Salisbury at the Foreign Office (he was also prime minister at the time). The rest is history.

Patrick became more and more convinced that mosquitoes carried malaria, but which mosquito and how? Malaria was one of the most destructive diseases ever known and credited for the decline of many ancient civilizations. He didn't know then that the malarial parasite was so small that contemporary microscopes could not easily detect it. Manson experimented like in the old days in Amoy, not resting until he had answers. It was quieter at night with few interruptions; even the garrulous parrot had gone to sleep. He applied for a grant to do research in British Guiana but failed to raise the money. Then in 1894 Surgeon Major Ronald Ross of the Indian Army turned up unexpectedly at Queen Anne Street and was invited up to the Muck Room to admire the parasites and learn of Manson's Mosquito-Malaria theory (the agent that causes malaria was spread by an insect). Ronald Ross had the advantage of being employed in the Indian Army. He didn't need a grant. The army put him on special duty and paid his salary for three years despite most senior members of the armed forces being of the opinion that the very idea of mosquitoes carrying malaria was absurd. Ross was sent to India in 1895 and started his research, examining passengers on the boat. Three years was hardly long enough. It didn't help that he was moved from place to place constantly, interrupting his research. Had it not been for Patrick's help and advice, he might not have made it. Many letters passed between them, with Manson offering advice, knowledge and encouragement. Ross, already adept at using the microscope, became even more skillful, finding different parasites inside different mosquitoes. His Indian patients, however, were reluctant to let a European doctor experiment on them. Patrick wrote, rather quaintly:

"Look upon your work as a Holy Grail and yourself as Sir Galahad and never give up the research."

Ross thought he had the wrong kind of mosquitoes – three kinds of malaria had been discovered and it was thought that each might require a different mosquito. He persisted in unbearable heat, the humidity turning his clothes and his microscope mouldy. Like Patrick in Amoy he felt isolated. Then, the final ignominy, he contracted malaria himself while out researching in the Nilgiri hills near Ootacamund. While he recovered slowly, the hunt continued with paid Indian researchers. Bottles of hatched Anopheles mosquitoes were brought in and fed on a willing patient who had malaria. On the 20th of August 1897 – now known as Mosquito Day – Ross spotted the malarial parasite in his patient's blood. He had matched the mosquito and the parasite. All the clues Manson had given him fitted.

Twenty hours later he had discovered greater numbers of the parasite. Their shape and movement were just as Manson had described. He had done it. He sat down and composed a poem for his wife. Ross's sideline was poetry.

This day relenting God
Hath placed within my hand
A wondrous thing; and God
Be praised. At His command
Seeking His secret deeds
With tears and toiling breath.
I find thy cunning seeds
Oh million-murdering Death
I know that this little thing
A myriad men will save –
O Death where is thy sting?
Thy Victory O grave?

Ross sent his preparations mounted in formalin and glycerine to Patrick, who was shooting grouse in Scotland. Patrick rushed back to London and cabled Ross. *"Congratulations, you are on the right track at last."*

The hunt became a race. Now it was a rush to see who would get there first. All the old rivalries emerged. The Italians, the French and the Americans were on the trail. Like the climb to be first on Mount Everest, it became a question of national pride. Meanwhile Ross continued his research using birds. Although they contracted malaria via a different mosquito, the transmission and life cycle were the same. Ross illustrated this in a beautifully drawn diagram he sent to Manson. The problem had been solved. Ross came home to England in 1899. However, the Colonial Office wanted this proved before spending large sums of money on screening buildings in its malaria-infested colonies. Here, the Italian Professor Grassi, who had done much work on malarial mosquitoes himself, obliged with an experiment. Two of Manson's students, an Englishman and an Italian, were sent to live in a specially built mosquito-proof hut in the Roman Campagna, on a hunting estate owned by King Umberto. Accompanied by two servants and an artist they spent the malarial months from July to October wandering freely in the marshes from sunrise to sunset. None of them got malaria in what was a high-risk area for the disease.

The hut became famous. The great and the good came to visit. Even King Umberto turned up. Patrick followed this up with his own experiment using mosquitoes sent by Professor Grassi from Rome. They arrived in a diplomatic bag from Brindisi and were fed on Patrick's twenty-three-year-old son Thurburn, then a student at Guy's Hospital. Within fifteen days Thurburn fell ill – he had two relapses later – but it now proved for certain that malaria was transmitted by mosquitoes. Despite this proof, many still refused to believe this, considering it blasphemous and against the will of God. They thought Manson not right in the head. One day as he was limping past the Athencum Club   he had a stick because of his gout – he happened to pass some doctors emerging after a good lunch. "Who is that?" one asked. "That is Mosquito Manson," said another, tapping his forehead with his finger. Manson retaliated in the same vein – tapping his forehead and sticking out his tongue. "We were all dotty," he said. Professor Grassi, in Italy, did not agree.

"I salute Manson who first formulated mosquito-malarial theory..."

In 1901 Manson, Ross and Grassi were proposed for a Nobel Prize. Ross won the award in 1902. He never acknowledged Manson's part in his success, even discrediting him openly. Had Manson not seen his tiny worms all those years ago in Amoy and traced their life cycle, it would have taken longer to solve the puzzle of malaria. Ross also fell out noisily with Professor Grassi. In 1912 Ross took libel actions against several colleagues, including Grassi and Manson. Manson had criticized the teaching at the Liverpool School of Tropical Medicine where Ronald Ross had been a professor. And in 1930, eight years after Patrick's death, Ross wrote a book, *Memories of Sir Patrick Manson*, in an attempt to belittle him. Malaria is still a scourge in the world today.

In 1898 Patrick published his bible of tropical medicine, *Manson's Tropical Diseases*, still widely used all over the world today. In 1899 the London School of Tropical Medicine was opened in an unprepossessing part of London close to the Albert Dock. This was the result of Patrick's persistence, the support of Joseph Chamberlain, Colonial Secretary, and a generous donation from Mr Bomanji Petit of Bombay. Not everyone agreed with the idea of a school for tropical medicine. Among Patrick's many honours was election as a Fellow of the Royal Society in 1900, followed by two prestigious knighthoods. As his reputation grew so did his income. Now he was earning £4,000–£5,000 a year from his private practice. These honours did not compensate for the loss of his son Thurburn in 1902 on an expedition to research beriberi on Christmas Island. Patrick continued with his research into diseases such as sleeping sickness and leishmaniasis, which his grandson, my father, Clinton, would carry on after him.

Patrick's greatest legacy was the London School of Tropical Medicine, an idea which had germinated in his mind since the founding of the Hong Kong School of Medicine. He had many admirers; he was always followed by crowds of eager students. But he also had enemies – no one in his position, as passionate and outspoken as he was, could escape the carping, vindictiveness and petty jealousies of the medical fraternity. As Patrick got older his gout worsened, sometimes restricting him to bed for weeks on end. Now he found it difficult to get around London or even up to his Muck Room but he managed a trip to America in 1905 and a visit to Cannes to treat the ailing King of Siam. He would travel to work by car with the blinds drawn to hide his pipe smoking and hobble with his stick around the ward, his bright eyes missing nothing. His dry Scottish wit – delivered in perfectly accented English or in broad Doric – never failed to entertain. There was, too, a cheerful family wedding. His daughter Edith, a nurse at the London Hospital, met an ambitious young doctor called Philip Bahr. The press reported that the bride wore white satin embroidered with empire wreaths and Louis bows with a full satin trail and a veil of Brussels lace, with orange blossom in her dark hair. Her bouquet was of exotic flowers, memories perhaps of China where she was born. There were nine bridesmaids in powder blue with bonnets trimmed with forget-me-nots and roses. A reception was held at the Langham Hotel.

After his retirement in 1912, Patrick visited Philip and Edith in Ceylon (Sri Lanka), where he shot a jungle fowl and examined it for parasites. He visited his daughter Violet in Southern Rhodesia (Zimbabwe). He had bought a small country retreat at Chalfont St Giles, where he took up gardening and carpentry. When this was sold he acquired a fishing lodge near Lough Mask in County Galway, where he suffered his first heart attack in 1921. Even when he couldn't walk, he was wheeled to the edge of the moor, still as good a shot as ever. Sometimes he was even pushed into the lough in his wheelchair to fish. He was popular with the locals and rode for miles into the hills visiting their sick. It was the locals who warned him that Sinn Fein were out to get him. Some of his papers went up in smoke when the lodge was burnt down after his death in 1922. Patrick died at home in London surrounded by his family. A memorial service was held in St Paul's and he was buried in Aberdeen, overlooking the River Dee where he had spent so many happy fishing hours. He was back where it had all started with frogs

Sir Patrick Manson with his grandsons Clinton and Hugh Manson-Bahr

and fish and wild cats, where he had seen his first intestinal worms. When he left for Takao in 1866 he could not have known how it would all end, with a legacy to the world, aided by the Empire, for he saw the Empire as a force for good. Ironically that same Empire helped transmit the malarial parasite through war and slavery as did the Romans who first brought the parasite to Europe.

Of medical research Patrick said, *"Most mistakes in medicine occur not from not knowing but from not looking."* His discovery that filariasis in humans is transmitted by mosquitoes is the foundation of modern tropical medicine. He is remembered as 'the Father of Tropical Medicine'.

THE SCOT AND THE PASHA

EGYPT 1805–1860

Interview with the Viceroy of Egypt at his palace in Alexandria in 1839
Painting by David Roberts/Heritage Image Partnership/Alamy stock photo

In 1805, during the Napoleonic Wars, another Scottish youth left his home in rural Aberdeenshire and made his way to Alexandria, where his older brother John was already established as a merchant. He found a wretched town full of scavenging dogs, beggars, dromedaries and that slave of animals, the donkey. There was one hotel run by a drunken Italian. The noisy mix of Turks, Arabs, Egyptians, Copts, Nubians and Bedouins, Jews, Greeks and Armenians was a culture shock after the sleepy town of Keith. Life in Alexandria was lived in the street. A French visitor called the city "the saddest and most deserted place in the world." But, however wretched the city, it offered opportunities for the twenty-year-old that his home couldn't match. The new viceroy, Muhammad Ali Pasha, was opening his country up to the world and inviting foreign investment. The Pasha was in a hurry to modernize and needed the skills of European merchants, doctors, scientists and engineers. Robert landed on his feet with a position as secretary to the British Consul and Political Agent, Major Missett. The major came to rely heavily on his young assistant since he suffered from a long-term degenerative disease. For Robert it was an introduction to the merchants and investors who poured through the consul's door.

Muhammad Ali Pasha had been given the governorship of Egypt (then part of the Ottoman Empire) as a reward for helping the Turks defeat Napoleon. Born Albanian in Macedonia, then under Turkish control, he had proved a brilliant military leader in their army. He didn't speak Arabic; Turkish was the language of the court. He had no love for the Moslem clergy but he welcomed all religions, commenting that, "It would be a misfortune if one was not correct." He despised the Ottoman Empire and his long-term plan was full independence from his Ottoman rulers, whereas the European powers wanted to keep the Empire intact. In 1811 the Pasha had dealt with a major threat to his power. It confirmed what many said, that the Pasha was an oriental despot. *The Times* agreed with them. The Mamelukes were an army of slave mercenaries, going back 600 years, who had grown powerful and corrupt under Ottoman rule. Taken as young boys from all around the Mediterranean and even as far away as north Persia and the Caucasus, they were highly trained, highly organized and adhered to a strict chivalric code similar to that of the Christian knights. They had seen off the Crusaders and even got the better of the Mongols. Now they had become immensely rich, owning most of the land in Egypt. The Pasha saw them as a threat. He invited 400 of their leaders to a ceremony at the Citadel, his palace fortress in Cairo. After a pleasant evening, as the visitors ambled cheerfully down the narrow passageway between the high walls, soldiers above opened up with muskets. No one survived. The heads were sent to Istanbul, the ears dispatched separately. Rosina, Robert's step-daughter, remembered seeing the heads carried through the streets on lances. She was five at the time. This became known as the Massacre of the Citadel. But the Pasha did not stop there. He hunted down the remaining 3,000 men, women and children.

This massacre horrified the British. Major Missett fully supported his government. Robert was fortunate in his choice of employer and friend. The major introduced him to Samuel Briggs, who ran the most successful trading firm in Alexandria. For sixty years, Briggs & Co represented British commercial interests in Egypt with the full support of the Pasha. It was the rock on which British commercial and political interests were built. Briggs & Co were said to have 'fingers in every pie'. Lord Palmerston commented that it represented a mere vested interest.

Robert joined the company in 1811, becoming a partner in the firm by 1821. As well as becoming a director of P&O, he held the Egyptian Transit Agreement covering the conveyance of passengers and goods from Alexandria to the Port of Suez for the onward route to India. This was a lucrative venture. The Pasha invested $100,000 in the transit company and took many of the profits. No doubt Robert did well too. In 1822 Samuel Briggs negotiated the sale of the Pigot Diamond, at 47 carats the largest in Europe. It is thought that the diamond was acquired by a member of the East India Company who sold it to the Pasha for £30,000. Five per cent of this went as commission to Briggs & Co. This was heady stuff and more exciting than working for a family linen company back home in Aberdeenshire. Not so pleasant was the backlash of the Turkish massacre of Greeks on the island of Chios at Easter the same year. Most of the island's population was wiped out, its women and children raped and taken as slaves. Many ended up in the markets of Cairo and Alexandria. The famous painting by Delacroix, *Scenes from the Massacre of Chios*, caused an outcry and encouraged philhellenes, including Lord Byron, to support Greek independence from Ottoman rule. This resulted in a war lasting eight years.

With the Mamelukes wiped out, the Pasha started to modernize. He built up an industrial base. He established a professional bureaucracy and medical schools, including one for women. This was unusual in a city where women were invisible. Since there were no suitably educated girls in Alexandria, he recruited young slave girls, probably Greek, and paid them well. Their tasks included vaccinating against smallpox, improving childbirth, treating syphilis. The Pasha wanted a higher and healthier birthrate to replace his army. Most children died before the age of three due to the mother's poor health and frequent childbearing. He also sent students to Europe to learn engineering, science and medicine. Not all his reforms were welcomed. He confiscated all the privately-owned land and introduced conscription. The peasants responded by maiming their children. Losing an eye or a limb seemed preferable to fighting in the army. But the Pasha got round this by founding a regiment for the disabled. After all, he said, you can still shoot with one eye.

Muhammad Ali Pasha was someone the British could do business with. Although he didn't admire their culture, he welcomed their skills. He wanted to emulate their navy and sent one of his sons to serve. Lady Jane Franklin, introduced to the Pasha by Robert, described him as "*a small vulgar-faced man with quick little eyes always in perpetual motion. His mouth expressed both humour and satire.*" He was fair with blue eyes, an expansive moustache and a beard as white and fluffy as a terrier's. His pantaloons were voluminous, his turban a white puffball, his slippers red and his long curving sword inlaid with gold. A wide cummerbund of shimmering gold silk made him look even stouter than he was. According to visitors, he kept a picture of Queen Victoria in his rooms and would sit in a chair and gaze at it fondly. Although not a religious man, the Pasha was careful not to neglect his duties. Every year he sent a silk carpet to Mecca to be draped over the Prophet's tomb, replacing the old one worn out by the kisses of the faithful. This was done with great ceremony and maximum publicity. A procession led by camels decorated with shells and ostrich feathers carried the carpet through the streets of Alexandria accompanied by dervishes and howling women trying to outdo the kettle drums and the shrieks of the mob. Every year it was the same. Every year the shrine received a new carpet.

In 1813 Robert married a young widow whose family came from Lambesc in France. Maria Piozin was the daughter of a French merchant in Istanbul. Her husband, Count Pierre Anthony Pellegrini di Tibaldi, doctor to Muhammad Ali Pasha, had died suddenly in unexplained circumstances. Rumour was that the doctor had been poisoned by the Pasha because of his objections to the Mameluke massacre. Maria brought her four children with her. Robert left his primitive bachelor home. According to subsequent tenants, the building leaked and had a foul stench. Visitors, of which there were many, had to sleep under the billiard table in wet weather. One aristocratic lady sheltered with her baby under an umbrella in one of the many winter storms. Later, when ten people died there, it was discovered that the house had been built over an open sewer.

In 1814, the year after his marriage, and the birth of his first son, the job of Consul General of Egypt became vacant. Robert applied but it went to Henry Salt, who was better qualified. Henry had travelled widely, spoke some Middle Eastern languages and had influential friends. He admired the Pasha for the stability he had brought to Egypt. "*Ali was extraordinary for a Turk*," he wrote to the Foreign Office. As well as his consular duties, Henry Salt had a profitable sideline in the acquisition of antiquities. A consul's pay was not generous. Salt was highly respected by his contemporaries and was a good friend to Robert. No one thought badly of him for this theft of cultural treasures. He worked on behalf of the British Museum and some aristocratic backers and accompanied William Bankes on a hunting trip up the Nile, where Bankes acquired a superb alabaster sarcophagus. But the bounty hunters paid a heavy price for their activities. They suffered from dysentery – some dying from it. There were scorpion bites, malaria – the cause of which was yet to be discovered by Manson – Robert's grandson-in-law – and, for those unwise enough to bathe in the Nile, bilharzia, although it too was undiscovered until the next century. Trachoma and syphilis were widespread. Gustav Flaubert's lasting memento of his Nile visit was syphilis. William Bankes suffered severe attacks of trachoma, which damaged his sight. Henry Salt was ill for many years and probably died of syphilis.

The French consuls were even more dependent on the sale of antiquities since their official salaries, although better, were not always paid on time. Ali Pasha facilitated these expeditions and took his cut. After all, it had been his idea to dismantle the pyramids in order to dam the Nile. Salt wasn't the only pursuer of antiquities.

Many nationalities joined the hunt. One of the most successful 'raiders' was an Italian, Belzoni, who removed the sarcophagus of Seti the First from his tomb and sold it to a collector. Some antiquities ended up in Russia on the River Neva. Among artefacts brought back to London was the head of Rameses II from Thebes shipped via Malta to London. In the eighteen years between 1828 and 1846, thirteen entire temples were lost. Not everyone approved of these thefts. Lord Byron spoke out against his fellow countrymen. Robert would have known of these activities. Briggs & Co shipped home the booty. The 1820s were good years too for trade with newly planted Egyptian cotton, much of which was exported to Liverpool. Egyptian grain fed the British regiments in Malta, Sicily and Spain. Muhammad Ali Pasha monopolized this trade, the profits of which funded his military campaigns. This wealth and the firm, if brutal, rule of the Pasha made Alexandria one of the most prosperous and exciting cities at the time. Its population had swollen with foreign immigrants and the migration of the peasants to the city. Society was mobile. Money was all that mattered. Europeans eyed their prospects greedily. Alexandria was an agreeable place to live, situated between the sea and the salt lake of Mareotis, except when the khamsin blew burning sand over the city. Summers were hot and humid, freshened by cooling breezes from the sea. Torrential storms in the winter sometimes brought hail, snow and floods. Despite the regular outbreaks of plague and cholera carried in by pilgrims to Mecca, the city grew prosperous. Hotels run by Maltese, Greeks, Spanish and even a boarding house owned by an English woman sprang up. A tram ran through the city and a ten-mile corniche followed the coast.

In 1833 Robert became British Consul in Alexandria, thanks to Samuel Briggs's influence. Consuls connected to Briggs & Co were favoured by the Pasha. Robert's success was bittersweet. His wife Maria had died five years previously in childbirth at the age of forty-three. In sixteen years of marriage to Robert she had endured ten pregnancies, with the loss of three babies. She left three daughters including twins, four sons all under twelve, and four older children from her first marriage. Maria's oldest daughter, Rosina, stepped in to care for the younger children with the help of servants, a housekeeper and an Italian butler. But it was a problem being a widower since a consul was expected to hold receptions and keep his home available for the British visitors who passed through. Some visitors were better company than others. Disraeli visited in 1831 and had an audience with the Pasha facilitated by Robert. Lady Hester Stanhope passed through in 1812. The Pasha became so infatuated he gave her a horse before asking for her hand in marriage. Despite her indigence, Lady Hester declined the offer. "Pray what is to become of Lady Stanhope's debts?" was a constant refrain in the consulate, who did not want to accept liability. Lady Talbot climbed up Pompey's column on a rope ladder and wrote a letter on the top. Lady Jane Franklin, widow of the arctic explorer, left a description of Robert. They had travelled up the Nile, with seven others, on a boat Robert had chartered for the trip. She described *"a singular and interesting-looking man, of I know not what age, slender and delicate-looking, awkward yet gentlemanly, yet having a very mild but intellectual countenance, and a manner which though timid and embarrassed, and indicative of a great absence of mind, is placid and contemplative."* Perhaps, like many Scots, Robert was not given to small talk or perhaps a little of Jane went a long way. She was known to be waspish and flattered no one. Demanding travellers like Jane were one of Robert's problems. There was a turbulent falling-out early in the trip and Jane abandoned ship with an Austrian missionary with whom she formed a close relationship.

As consul, Robert attended regular meetings with the other foreign consuls at the Pasha's palace at Ras-al-Tin – the Garden of the Figs. Built on the coast in Italian rococo style topped by Moorish towers, it had thirteen acres of gardens with orange groves, sycamores and mimosa, tended by two Scottish gardeners.

A painting by the artist David Roberts shows the Pasha reclining at one end of a large red divan, his body turned towards the harbour where his fleet is moored. The competing consuls, including Robert, sit at the far end waiting their turn. Robert is wearing his consul's uniform with its outsize epaulettes. One observer commented that *"the Pasha was surrounded, flattered and cajoled by a set of foreign adventurers."* Of all these adventurers, the French were the preferred advisors. As well as his consular duties, Robert was expected to act like a travel agent. Expectations were high. There was horse riding in the desert, picnics by the pyramids and parties in the consulate. That these tourists were people of wealth and influence made them even more demanding.

Robert was easily accessible, for he lived in the Place des Consuls, a newly built square near the sea. Imposing mansions with classical facades and Venetian shutters surrounded a park

Place des Consuls, Alexandria, 19ᵗʰ-century engraving
Old Book Images/Alamy stock photo

with trees, a pond and a statue of Muhammad Ali Pasha on horseback. This was the fashionable part of the city, home to wealthy merchants. Every morning at sunrise the National Guard turned up like an alarm clock to drill in the square. During the day, smart carriages furnished with well-dressed ladies drove up and down the boulevards while the men sweated in their tailcoats and hats. All the different nationalities, Greek, Armenian, French, Italian and British, were served by their own churches. There were also two convents, and a European Hospital. The Thurburns retained their country house, the Sycamores on the Mahmoudia Canal, a choice residential location despite the smell of the night soil awaiting collection and the corpses of dead animals. A hedge and a border of sycamores managed to keep these odours at bay. This didn't deter some residents from lowering buckets into the canal for water. The six-acre garden

Mahmoudia Canal, Alexandria
Pump Park Vintage Photography/Alamy stock photo

with fruit trees, myrtle, jasmine, oleanders, dates and pomegranates offered a cool escape from the city. You could sit in the rose arbours and watch the boats making their way to the Nile, past the wheat and cotton fields on the opposite bank, knowing that much of the cargo and passengers travelled courtesy of Thurburn and Briggs.

This was only possible since the construction of the canal, which linked Alexandria to Cairo for the 80-mile desert crossing to Suez, where the P&O steamers waited to carry travellers on to Calcutta. It was said that 23,000 labourers died during the first ten months, digging the canal with their bare hands.

One of the more exotic visitors to the country house was the explorer Richard Burton, who turned up in full Arab gear. He put his tent among the myrtle and oleanders and spent a month reading the Koran preparing for his pilgrimage to Mecca. Unlike Jane, he spoke warmly of Robert. Robert and his son-in-law acquired a passport for Burton in the name of an Indo-British subject called Dr Abdullah. Burton survived his visit and was the first European to successfully make the Haj. Robert was also an active member of the newly created Board of Health, which ran the European Hospital in the Place des Consuls, funded by private subscription with a small contribution from the British government. Like his future grandson-in-law Patrick Manson, Robert took an interest in public health, advocating better drains and cleaner water. Perhaps he remembered that sewer under his house and its ten victims.

In 1831 a terrible plague struck Egypt, carried in by pilgrims from Mecca. Plagues arrived regularly but this one lasted forty months, leaving ghost towns echoing with the wailing of the mourners; 40,000 died in Alexandria. The consulates closed, ships were marooned, despite Robert's objections to the severe quarantine rules, which threatened trade. The locals, too, failed to observe the rules despite the Pasha threatening to cut off their heads. It didn't stop them from burying bodies beneath their floorboards or throwing them into the canal in the dead of night. Although Alexandria was used to dealing with epidemics, this was the most destructive and caused lasting economic damage. In Cairo one third of the city's population died in the same outbreak. This pandemic came after a disastrous war for the Pasha. The Greek War of Independence had lasted for eight years. It was seven years since the massacre at Chios. Much of Greece was still under Turkish domination. The European powers were united in their condemnation of Turkey's occupation of Greece. The British public sided with the Greeks. The Pasha was in a difficult position. He didn't need a costly war that risked his newly created navy, equipped by Thurburn and Briggs. On the other hand he had gained Crete as part of a deal with his Ottoman rulers and he couldn't refuse to support them. He sent his son Ibrahim with 16,000 men to help the Turks control the Peloponnese, but despite the terrible atrocities committed by Ibrahim's army, they failed to secure Crete. The fleets gathered at Navarino, a large natural harbour on the west coast. Although the allied Turkish and Egyptian fleets outnumbered the European allies, their boats were small with old-fashioned guns. On the 13th of October 1827 the British Admiral Codrington sailed into the bay to face the Ottomans. He had planned this as a show of force and not a precursor to battle. But a week later allied warships from Britain, Russia and France followed accompanied by a noisy brass band. The subsequent battle was intense and ended with the destruction of most of the Ottoman fleet. Casualties were horrendous but in the Peloponnese and the whole of Greece, church bells rang and bonfires illuminated the mountains like giant candles. The Greeks were free at last after 371 years of Ottoman rule. The Cretans, however, who had suffered so terribly under Ibrahim Pasha, remained part of the Ottoman Empire until 1897. Of Muhammad Ali Pasha's precious navy, only fourteen ships made it home, and 8,000 sailors died.

The defeat at Navarino brought another influx of Greek slaves into Alexandria. Some were repatriated to Greece. Others found life to their taste and married their purchasers. One English visitor bought his Cretan wife in the market at Alexandria. Although slavery had been abolished in 1833, it continued in Egypt. Most slaves came from the Sudan and Ethiopia. They were sold regularly in the markets. Slavery was openly practised in Egypt. The Pasha's troops were paid in slaves and every September troops went into the Nubian mountains for an annual slave hunt. Between 1820 and 1835, it was said that Nubians were being trafficked at a rate of 10,000 a year. William Bankes was shocked when he saw a boat on the Nile "crammed full of black baby slaves" en route to Cairo. British companies knew about the trade; there is no record of the Thurburns being involved, although one of their family companies was involved in the ivory trade and it was widely known that slaves were used to obtain the ivory.

Some observers considered slavery in Egypt to be 'kinder' than the European variety since slaves' duties tended to be domestic. They were able to gain their freedom and become important personages in their own right. Some assumed the status of their owners. One visitor to the Sultan in Istanbul was kept waiting while two haughty black giants commented rudely on his appearance. A slave's life seemed preferable to that of the peasants, who were heavily taxed and forced to work unpaid on public works like the Mahmoudia Canal. These were the real victims of the Pasha's economic miracle. Although Clot Bey, the Pasha's French physician and the only doctor to remain at his post during the plague epidemic, remarked that the Egyptian diet of sorghum bread, beans, chickpeas, lentils and vegetables was healthy, there wasn't enough of it to go around. Many Egyptians starved.

No doubt the nine-year-old boy Robert discovered in the slave market in Alexandria in 1835 would not have agreed that Egyptian slavery was kind. When Robert found the youth, he had already passed through nine owners and travelled over 2,000 miles from his home in the Sudan. Robert bought the boy and took him home to the house in the Place des Consuls, where the terrified child (he thought that Europeans would eat him) was washed and given a clean set of clothes. Selim Aga was a Nubian from a warrior tribe called the Taqali, who lived in the hills of Darfur, the son of a prosperous farmer, and had been kidnapped tending his father's goats. He was six when he was taken. The large, luxurious Thurburn house would have been terrifying with its many rooms, its books and paintings and noisy population of children. The housekeeper who cleaned Selim Aga up was kind, as was the Italian butler, but the boy could converse with neither for he spoke only Taqali with a smattering of Arabic picked up on his journey. Shortly after his arrival, the boy accompanied John and Robert and their families, together with the housekeeper and the Italian butler, to Scotland. Robert had asked for a leave of absence. The summer heat didn't suit him and he seems to have suffered some on-going health problems. The family took the slow route home, visiting the tribe of Thurburns scattered throughout the Mediterranean, including an Italian Thurburn, an illegitimate son of John's. They travelled by boat to Malta, Messina, Naples, Genoa, then by carriage to Milan and across Europe to Rotterdam, where they crossed the channel to England. They moved up to Scotland where John had built a handsome residence in 1823 at Peterculter near Aberdeen. The house sat with its walled garden in thirteen acres surrounded by forty acres of pasture. It overlooked the River Dee towards the distant Grampians. With the mild microclimate the family grew peaches outdoors. There was shooting, and fishing on the estate. At the time, Murtle was considered one of the finest estates in South East Scotland. Robert spent seven months based here, placing his children in schools in Britain. When he returned to Egypt, he left Selim at Murtle under the care of his sister-in-law Elizabeth.

The boy attended the local school and learnt to read and write in English – he even wrote poems. He liked to look out of the large

Murtle House, Peterculter, Aberdeenshire, home of John Thurburn

dining room windows, over the fields and the walled garden towards the river, and compose poems. In his 'Ode to Britain' he wrote in flowery words his praise for the country that had rescued him:

> *Britain, thou land of peace and joy,*
> *How strong thy bulwarks are;*
> *Thou standest far above the world,*
> *And that without a par.*
> *They hail thee as the stranger's home,*
> *The freedom of the slave,*
> *Thy motto is – 'Where'er I go,*
> *The captive I will save.'*

The novelist Sarah Harriet Burney, half-sister of Fanny, declared that the boy sang Scottish ballads like a nightingale. Later, Selim accompanied John Thurburn on his travels in Europe, Asia, Africa and South America. He published a book, lectured in the Great Exhibition in 1851 and petitioned Lord Palmerston for a trans-

Africa east-west railway. He eventually became secretary to Richard Burton on his travels in West Africa. Burton, who had scant respect for Africans, was fulsome in his praise of Selim, describing him as:

"honest, civil, unpresuming, could cook, doctor, carry out carpentry and gardening, shoot and stuff birds, and was very competent in taking meteorological records, and generally took all the trouble of life off my hands."

Later, Selim worked for other travellers. He came to a sticky end murdered by a tribe in Liberia, who allowed him one last prayer before slicing off his head. Selim loved the damp Scottish countryside and had hoped to retire to a cottage near Murtle. His descendants remain in Scotland.

Before returning to Egypt in 1836, Robert and his partner Samuel Briggs called on Lord Palmerston in London to lobby for extra staff expenses for the consulates in Egypt and Syria. Robert was constantly complaining to the Foreign Office about his low salary of £300 a year. Lord Palmerston said that if he didn't like it, he could leave. It was no loss. After all, Robert had his own commercial interests. All those fees for introductions to the royal family and the commercial concessions he organized brought in a healthy income. Still, a consul's work was onerous and time-consuming: dealing with mail transfers to India, procuring coal for the fleet, lobbying against duties levied on British goods, monitoring the coming and going of British boats, dealing with the problems of British sailors and visitors, managing the many pandemics, and welcoming demanding tourists. Robert's boss, Colonel Campbell, the consul general in Cairo, backed him up, adding that the British had more work and more visitors than any other consuls despite being paid less. The French and Austrian consulates were better staffed and better paid. This conversation was on-going and many letters were written about it. Eventually Robert's pay rose to £450 a year. Samuel and

Robert continued to be vociferous supporters of the Pasha. Robert was especially close to him. It was well known that Briggs & Co had attempted to guide British policy in the Levant in the interests of the Pasha. There is no doubt they had flourished as the Pasha's commercial agent in Britain but that there was certainly a conflict of interest between Robert's position as consul and his work as a partner in a major mercantile company. It was accepted that British consuls could have commercial interests but there were limits. The visit did not go down well. Robert returned to Egypt empty-handed. It was unlikely that a man who forced the Chinese to accept the opium trade would change his policies for a Scottish consul in Alexandria.

Robert made his way home via Florence. Social life resumed with weddings and parties among the different communities. These were expensive and theatrical affairs, held at night in jasmine-scented courtyards lit by painted glass lanterns. Nightingales sang in cages and fountains trickled their precious water. Tables sagged under the weight of their silver. What was the point of making money if you couldn't show it off? And Alexandria was the place to boast. Besides, these events helped promote British interests. A conscientious consul made sure he knew the right people and attended the important occasions. One of the most important was the wedding of Zeynab Khanoum, the Pasha's youngest and favourite daughter. No expense was spared, although the bride was unhappy with her father's choice of groom. She wore silk with Brussels lace and a velvet jacket trimmed with sable. So many and so heavy were her diamonds that she looked like a Christmas tree. At the sit-down banquet, cutlery was provided for everyone to please the European guests. The Pasha seemed unconcerned that the theatrical production in Italian offended religious sensitivities. He was no friend of the mullahs. After the lengthy celebrations the bride was transported to her husband's house with trays of jewels and clothes carried through the city on the heads of soldiers. Mounted eunuchs escorted them to the noisy accompaniment of cannons and kettledrums. The bride wasted no time finding pleasure with a retinue of lovers. The Coptic weddings were altogether more gloomy affairs, with chanting that lasted for hours, relieved only by musicians including the Almé, Alexandria's famous singing women. The Coptic women too were secluded and wore veils. A European visitor described how the brides, some as young as twelve, sought comfort during the ceremonies in the arms of their black nurses. The Copts considered daughters 'a lump of grief' to be married off as early as possible.

A new form of tourism emerged as a result of the harem literature that was much in vogue in Europe. Wealthy women from Britain turned up expecting to meet the veiled ladies and demanded that the consul set up meetings for them. Sophia Poole, author of a collection of letters, *The Englishwoman in Egypt 1842–1844*, was scathing of the harem women. They were, she said, "*uneducated with minds like untidy gardens.*" One day she witnessed a stampede of the imperial gardens by a gaggle of women let out of their cage. They trampled the flower beds and devoured the fruit, much to the distress of the Scottish gardener. Inside the harem things were more organized, with clean and pleasant rooms simply furnished with large Turkish carpets and cushioned divans and, most essential, a husband's chair. The beds were more individual. One made of solid silver had pink satin coverlets and matching tulle mosquito nets. Sophia Poole was entertained to lunch by a princess, once a Circassian slave. The meal, accompanied by singers and dancers, consisted of many courses, salads, meat, breads, sweet meats, soups flavoured with rosewater, cherry water served in melon-shaped gold and silver cups. At first glance the princess seemed to have everything: beauty, elegance, clothes of cashmere and silk, diamonds that hung like ringlets in her hair. But when her guests commented on the size of her rooms, the princess wiped her beautiful eyes.

"Ah, your Queen can go out but I should be dead if they did not give me a large room for this is the only place I have to walk in."

In 1839 life became more difficult for Robert when the Turkish sultan attacked the Pasha's forces in Syria. The Pasha had acquired parts of Syria in an earlier war against the Ottomans. Now the Ottomans invaded to regain their lost territories. The war, a climax in a long struggle between the Pasha and his Ottoman rulers, threatened to destabilize the whole of the Middle East and risk war in Europe. The British, Russians and Austrians supported the Ottomans, whereas the French and the Spanish were allied to the Pasha. The Pasha sent his army to Syria under the command of his son Ibrahim. The Ottomans proved a pushover. Soldiers defected; the navy mutinied. Then the Sultan died suddenly in Istanbul, leaving his sixteen-year-old son as heir. The Ottomans, now in a weak position, offered to cede Syria to the Pasha but the British, Russians and Austrians forced them to withdraw the offer. The British sent a warship but there was little they could do against the 15,000 Egyptian troops based in Syria. Lord Napier took it upon himself to negotiate a deal with the Pasha without the agreement of Lord Palmerston. A collapse of Egypt was not in anyone's interests. The deal stated that the Pasha would give Syria, Palestine, Arabia and Crete back to the Sultan with what remained of his navy. In return the Pasha would gain control of Egypt and the Sudan in perpetuity. Robert still campaigned vigorously for the Pasha. He supported a strong independent Egypt as a counter-weight to the Russians, who sought to control the Ottomans. The Ottoman Empire was old and in decline. Robert assured Lord Palmerston that the Pasha was sound and loyal to Britain. Lord Palmerston did not agree. There were rumours that the Pasha had flirted with the Russians. Attempts to harm the Pasha's reputation in the British press alarmed Robert and spurred his campaign. It did him no favours. He retired suddenly.

The next consul, his son-in-law John Larking, was dismissed in 1841, accused of being too close to a family with mercantile interests (he was married to the beautiful Rosina, Robert's step-daughter). The British residents in Alexandria protested fiercely but the British government didn't want consuls with conflicting interests. Egypt was important as the route to India, especially when the railway from Alexandria to Cairo was completed under the direction of British engineer Robert Stephenson in 1856. (Robert had been involved with the negotiations.) In 1857 it was used to transport British troops to India to quell the mutiny during which one of Robert's sons narrowly escaped being butchered. The canal was completed by the French in 1869. The Pasha was not alive to see its completion. He died senile in 1848, leaving his empire to his grandson Abbas, a devout Muslim. The Pasha, declared Abbas, had been a slave to the foreign consuls. As the Pasha himself had said at the beginning,

> *"Without the English for my friends, I can do nothing. I foresaw long ago that I could undertake nothing grand without her permission. Wherever I turn, she (Queen Victoria) is there to baffle me."*

Robert, who was fifty-five in 1839, still had the energy to create a new business with his son-in-law. Unlike his brother John he showed no interest in retiring to Scotland despite his dislike of the Egyptian summers. His life in Alexandria included a family of sons- and daughters-in-law. His own sons were scattered; only one remained in Egypt. Perhaps he wanted to be near his wife's grave and those of four of his children. Or perhaps he could not retire as grandly as his brother, or had his defence of the Pasha tarnished his reputation back home? He had arrived in Alexandria at the age of twenty and had spent most of his life there. Egypt was not a British colony, so there were fewer rules on race and caste and fewer class distinctions. Here anyone could prosper, even drummer boys like

Donald Donald of the 78th Highlanders, who was captured during the Napoleonic Wars. Offered death or conversion by the Egyptians, Donald wisely chose the latter. When offered his freedom, he decided he was better off in Egypt, where he had prospered. Robert seemed settled. His stepchildren spoke French, Italian, English and some Arabic. His daughters had married well. One son had joined the business in Alexandria. The other three joined the navy, the army and the East India Company. Robert lost his most important supporter, the Pasha, who died demented in 1848. It was now time for that private holiday up the Nile with his family without an irate Jane Franklin or those pesky tourists who had poured through his doors. The Nile was not yet overrun with visitors. These came later thanks to Thomas Cook, whose first steamer was rented from the Pasha's grandson in 1860.

Travelling on the Nile wasn't easy. You didn't just pay your money and turn up. First you had to find your boat, sink it for two days to remove the vermin, then lift it out, dry, clean, paint and furnish it. For this you needed a competent dragoman. Robert's butler took on the task, hiring the cooks, cleaners, rowers and sailors – there could be as many as fifteen servants sleeping on deck. The boat was a dahabiya, a houseboat. In Arabic dahabiya meant 'golden boat', a reference to the boat used by Cleopatra and Julius Caesar, the earliest known tourists on the Nile. It was like a small dhow, with masts fore and aft, large crossed sails and was well kitted out with two decks. The top covered by an awning was for eating and relaxing. There were three cabins below, all wood-panelled with shutters to keep out the sand during storms. They didn't always work – Egyptian sand was as fine as flour. The large cabin had two beds and there were two single cabins separated by an open area furnished with divans and cupboards, which could serve as extra sleeping space. Cooking was done in a tiny kitchen at the front of the boat. Food hung in baskets on the upper deck. Meat and fish hunted from the boat were

A dahabiya Nile boat, Egypt
Colaimages/Alamy stock photo

supplemented by locusts, crocodile eggs, cranes, ducks, partridges and wild geese. The *Handbook for Travellers in Egypt*, published seven years after Robert's trip, told its readers to bring guns to shoot dinner. Live sheep and chickens were useful. English cheese was thought to be a good thing. Other necessary equipment were bedsteads, carpets, rat traps and washing tubs, and perhaps a piano as well, although the boatmen doubled as musicians – drumming and singing as required.

Women were advised to dress plainly, wear veils, gloves, and carry umbrellas. As the boat set off, a flag was hoisted to show the nationality of the travellers. Robert was accompanied by his step-daughter Rosina, her husband John, and their Italian butler. Other travellers joined them from time to time. Although Robert failed to leave a memoir of his travels, other travellers left diaries, including

Florence Nightingale with her *Letters from Egypt*. Florence had come to escape company and complained about the constant socializing at dusk when the boats would moor together and there would be parties with music and fireworks and chatter long into the night. Guests could lie on divans on the upper deck and watch the storks flying over the river at dusk. There were geese too, pelicans and purple cranes and orange and lilac sunsets that bled into the star-filled skies. The boat glided past the tantalizing shapes of ruins still concealed under centuries of shifting sand. The green fringe of tall date palms that lined the banks concealed the wilderness beyond. Some travellers found this landscape disturbing. All that empty space made them nostalgic for the comforting greens of England. Perhaps the mosquitoes and the dysentery most of them suffered made them wonder why they had undertaken such a journey in a boat without a proper lavatory.

Like many British visitors, Florence, only twenty-nine at the time, had not come to explore contemporary Egypt. It was ancient Egypt that attracted the tourists. She confided her feelings to her diary. She hated the dirt and the poverty, the begging and most of all the situation of the women who were treated worse than donkeys. Many tourists agreed. The elegant palms, fluffy tamarisk and yellow mimosa lent the villages a romantic air dispelled by further exploration. These villages of sun-dried mud houses with their palm-leaf roofs provided shops, porters, donkeys, food, blacksmiths, barbers and women. Old men smoking their shisha pipes and barefoot children waited for the boats to moor before rushing to sell trinkets. Florence wanted ruins without the hawkers. She thought the people savages. Behind the villages and before the encroaching desert were fields of wheat, tobacco and sugar cane irrigated by the Nile. Wild animals were abundant, enormous hyenas who left their footprints in the sand, dancing gazelles, antelopes, jackals, wild donkeys, hares and guinea fowl. There were reputed to be lions. Snakes and scorpions took their toll – some tourists were killed by bites. At Kom Ombo, on a bend in the river, crocodiles massed as they did in ancient times by the temple that was dedicated to them. All the visitors went home with souvenirs. Some took bits of mummies, a toe perhaps or a finger. Others, like William Bankes, removed stuccoes from the temples. One young girl discovered a hidden tomb with friezes and bas reliefs as fresh as the day they were painted. Robert acquired small objects. When Henrietta Isabella, my great-grandmother, died in 1938, her will listed a coin of Cleopatra, 12th-dynasty scarabs of cornelian and amethyst, an 18th-century scarab, a 12th-dynasty amethyst and cornelian necklace, a necklace of porcelain cats and a Greek pendant with a relief of Bacchus. Many of the sites we know today were buried in silt and some had villages built on top of them. And not only were the remains Egyptian, but there were also Roman and Greek temples as well as Byzantine churches.

After roaming the ruins, travelling there on donkeys, the tourists returned to their boats, relaxing on deck, drinking coffee, writing up their notes, painting water colours, admiring the sunset, playing cards or just chatting. The more energetic raced camels in the desert. An extraordinary mix of people and nationalities visited the Nile. It was on all wealthy Americans' wish lists. It was the celebrity safari of its time. Some did it in style. Lord Belmore brought his whole family, including his chaplain, doctor, nurses and cooks. He spent his time on clandestine excavations. The Duke of Hamilton was so impressed by the tombs that he had himself mummified Egyptian-style after death and buried in his mausoleum in Scotland. David Roberts, the artist, spent eleven months travelling and produced 300 images, which shaped British ideas of the Middle East. Most tourists went as far as the First Cataract. The longest stays were at Luxor, where you could buy jewellery, cartouches and body parts. If the winds were right the boats might carry on for another fortnight to the Second Cataract. Travelling upriver was slow and required rowing or towing. On the return journey the boats were carried downstream on the current.

Robert returned refreshed to Alexandria. He was still in business. But under Abbas, the Pasha's grandson, the British were no longer treated favourably. Egypt returned to conservative rule. Many of the Pasha's reforms were overturned. Robert's old partner Samuel Briggs died in 1853. In 1860, on his way back to Britain, Robert died suddenly in Lyon at the age of seventy-six. His body was shipped to Dover where he was buried. The mystery was that he died intestate, leaving his oldest son James Ptolemy to deal with the estate. James Ptolemy had joined the navy at the age of fifteen and spent his life sailing the oceans to enforce the end of the slave trade. Although slavery was abolished in Britain in 1807, it continued in many parts of the world.

After 1815 the Royal Navy had taken up the thankless task of patrolling the oceans. This was a risky venture. It was a war that lasted thirty years. The Royal Navy had its own slave history. Slaves had been used in its Caribbean dockyards and some officers owned plantations. But the mood in Britain was supportive of the Navy's actions. Prizes were offered for the ships that captured the most slavers. James Ptolemy served on the East African coast, where slaves had been transported to Arabia, Iran and India for centuries. He also patrolled the East Indies, the Pacific, the Mediterranean, the East Coast of America and commanded a ship in Rio de Janeiro where the Royal Navy successfully ended the Brazilian trade, Brazil being the largest importer of slaves. Between 1808 and 1860, 1,600 slave ships were captured and more than 150,000 Africans saved at the cost of the lives of many British crewmen. You could trace James Ptolemy's voyages by the birth places of his children and his holiday leaves. Not until the end of his life did he settle in London, where he died at ninety-one. At his death Robert was listed as having an address near Queen Anne Street, where his granddaughter Henrietta Isabella lived with her husband Patrick Manson and where his great-granddaughter Edith Manson married Philip Bahr forty-nine years later in 1909.

Commander James Ptolemy Thurburn
National Maritime Museum Images, Greenwich, London

HERE COME THE GERMANS

RUSSIA 1787–1904

The Blessig family in West Derby

In the 19ᵗʰ century, English Quay was one of the most prestigious residential streets in St Petersburg. When Philippe Jacques Blessig left his native Alsace in 1787 to try his luck in the cold, desolate city, he never imagined that within twenty-six years he would own a palace overlooking the River Neva. Philippe Jacques was the youngest son of an innkeeper in Strasbourg. His ancestors were master masons who had moved there in the 17ᵗʰ century from Vasselmheim on the river Mossig. Alsace was French and the family were French citizens who spoke both French and German. They became known as Blessig of the Axe after acquiring the Inn of the Axe in 1746. Seventeen-year-old Philippe Jacob started work as a commission merchant in Strasbourg. But the hoped-for prospects didn't materialize and, as the youngest son in a large family, there was little hope of any inheritance. So he decided to seek his fortune in Russia, which, under Catherine the Great, welcomed German and Baltic migrants.

When Philippe Jacques arrived in 1787, St Petersburg had existed for only eighty-four years. Peter the Great had chosen this unprepossessing site for its position on the Gulf of Finland and access to the Baltic. It was not an obvious choice for a capital city, being so far from anywhere. Thousands of serfs and prisoners died building this dream. There were problems with drainage and contaminated water causing regular epidemics of cholera and typhoid. Flooding, mists, fog and extremes of climate tested human endurance. Winter lasted from October to April and brought frosts of minus 60°C and four hours of daylight. During the twenty-two-hour days of summer the temperatures rose to 40°C. No Russians wanted to live in this godforsaken swamp. The foreigners, however, English, Dutch, German, Swedish, saw good prospects in this icy 'wild west' and moved in, encouraged by Catherine the Great, who was German.

At first, living conditions were difficult. The houses were small since the soil could not support anything more substantial. Made of wood with birch wood floors, they had double walls, windows and doors to keep out the cold. Huge ceramic stoves set into the interior walls warmed several rooms simultaneously using birch from the surrounding forests. Later houses were built of brick stucco (there was no building stone) and painted in bright colours to stand out in the blinding snow. Every summer, armies of workmen descended on the city to repair the subsidence, the cracks and the damp. As more people moved in, the islands in the delta were absorbed into the city and built on. On Vassili Ostrov (known as Basil Island), Peter the Great had built a Dutch town complete with canals. It appealed to the wealthy merchants, including Philippe Jacques, who built his first house there. In the winter when the river froze and the pontoon bridge was removed, the island was cut off for six months and accessible only on foot, preferably on skates.

Work was easy to find in this outpost of the Russian Empire. Philippe secured a position in the office of a Baltic German. After five years he took over the business, changing its name to Blessig & Co. According to the class system in Russia at the time, merchants were classified as serfs. The law was changed and, after approval from the Minister of the Interior, Philippe Jacques became Philip Ivanovitch, an honorary Russian citizen and 12th grade noble. At thirty-three he married a twenty-three-year-old Dutch girl, one of five daughters of a mercantile family, and bought a large dacha in Ligovo on the road to Peter the Great's summer retreat, Peterhof. His new estate, a long narrow strip of grassland and woods, stretched down to the Gulf of Finland. Unfortunately, Catharina, his wife, did not live long enough to enjoy this prosperity. She bore four children before dying at forty. Several women in the Blessig family seem to have died young. In the photos they sit forlornly in dark rooms, weighed down by their heavy clothes and pregnancy. It was said that the climate in St Petersburg was unhealthy and families who lived there grew weaker over the generations, or perhaps they succumbed to tuberculosis, which was common among all classes. Despite this, the Blessig family flourished. Some became scientists and doctors. Two became eye surgeons, one of whom was the foremost eye surgeon of his day in Russia, acquiring the august title of 'Excellency'.

Philip Ivanovich wasted no time marrying again. His eighteen-year-old bride, the niece of his previous wife, bore him another five children. Business was good. He established an office in Moscow, although staff had to travel the 400 miles between the cities by sleigh. Now an established merchant, he served as Consul General for the Duchy of Oldenburg in Germany. It was at this time that he bought the palace on English Quay where the family would live for the next fifty years. The Quay was home to European merchants and Russian aristocrats and was known as Les Promenades des Anglais. There were many English residents in St Petersburg. One English inhabitant of the Quay became an admiral in Catherine the Great's navy. The Scottish Greig family lived there for over 100 years and served the tsars as generals and government ministers. Of the two Scottish physicians in the street, one became personal physician to three tsars. The banking family Cazalet owned factories, a brewery, processing plants and a palace on the Quay. Foreigners, including 45,000 Germans, controlled about 97% of Russia's import and export trade by 1847. The Blessig palace was one of many on the embankment facing the River Neva.

Philip's son Philip Jacob was born here in 1821, the last of five children from his father's second marriage. At the time, the Cathedral of St Isaac was being built behind the house, its great dome rising slowly above the roof line. Behind the cathedral, canals and rivers snaked their way into the city. Work continued for forty years, lasting all of Philip Jacob's childhood. The noise of 25,000

Mansion on English Quay, St Petersburg
Yulia Babkina/Alamy stock photo

piles being driven into the marsh must have been trying, as was the construction of a neo-classical senate nearby. No. 3 English Quay was one of the smaller mansions in the long line of palaces that stretched along the river. Next door at No. 4, in an imposing mansion with classical columns, lived the Countess Laval with her library of 5,000 books. Her literary salons were famous, attended by celebrities such as Pushkin and Lermontov. In 1840, a ball there ended with a duel leading to the exile of Lermontov. It was at one of the palaces further along the Quay that Pushkin fell out with his wife's alleged lover and ended up killed in a duel. Countess Laval's daughter Princess Trubetskoy was exiled to Siberia with her Decembrist husband. Had they held their secret meetings here next door to the Blessigs? Other neighbours included grand dukes, princes and barons, including Baron von Stieglitz known as the Russian Rothschild and a good friend of the Blessigs.

The Blessig mansion was built around two interior courtyards. The main apartments, including a large dining room used for entertaining, overlooked the river at the front. Behind were offices, servants' quarters and kitchens. Family rooms at the rear, built around a second courtyard, housed members of the family and stables for the carriage and horses. Although the palace seemed spacious, it was fully occupied, with an extended family of adults, children, stepchildren, grandchildren and an army of servants including a housekeeper, Mademoiselle Europaus, sent by a charity that trained foundling children in domestic skills. Everyone walked past the windows of No. 3. It was a regular route for promenaders, including the Tsar and his court. In summer, boats moored alongside the Quay and in winter the frozen river would sparkle with the myriad fires of the ice fairs.

Blessig & Co had become important players in the growing import and export trade, although dealing with Russians required patience as their business methods were said to be 'oriental'. The winter months when the port froze brought some respite from work and allowed pleasures like shooting parties in the woods to hunt woodcock, wildfowl, black game, bears and wolves. There were skating parties, snow-shoeing, troika races and ice-hilling. Large blocks of ice were hacked out of the Neva and laid on a wooden frame to create an artificial hill about thirty feet high. The ice was then polished until it looked like glass. The toboggans waited on the top and, when the surface was slippery enough, slid down to the bottom where hot coffee was served before everyone scrambled up the hill to do it all over again. Ice-hilling parties were a favourite winter treat. Urban pleasures included the opera and the theatre.

The summer and autumn were busy months for the business. Before the railways, mail ships arrived and left twice a week. These were called 'post-days' when the pressure was full on. At the weekends the family escaped to their dacha, where they lived the life of a Chekhov play, swimming in the lakes, foraging for mushrooms and riding across their land to the sea. For Russians mushroom hunting was a sacred pastime. During Lent, mushrooms replaced meat. In the long summer dusks known as 'the white nights' when the sun never set, the family sat on their verandah smoking and listening to the nightingales. A favourite room was the large conservatory which housed orange and lemon trees, myrtle, castor oil plants and oleanders. In winter, the plants were wrapped in straw and, with their own hot water bottles, bundled into carriages on sledge runners and transported to the house on English Quay. Here they were displayed, a Mediterranean garden in the front windows overlooking the Neva where everyone could admire them. It was here in 1917 on this embankment that the ship *Aurora* fired the shot that signalled the storming of the Winter Palace during the Russian Revolution.

All the Blessig children were fluent in several languages. They learnt German from their parents, Russian from their nurses and friends, and English and French at school. Two boys graduated from St Petersburg University and two from Dorpat University in Estonia. The daughters went to boarding schools in the city. Their father, Philippe Jacques, now Philip Ivanovitch, died in 1832 and was buried in the Smolensky Cemetery with his first wife. The brothers sat down to work out the running costs of their house, with its army of servants, widowed wives and spare sisters. Despite their wealth the family was careful with its money, although they were generous benefactors to charities and cultural and educational organizations. The early death of wives and the remarrying of even younger ones led to large families so that even the house on English Quay became crowded. Perhaps Philip Jacob remembered a Russian proverb, "*all dogs cannot gnaw at one bone*", and realized that as a junior member of his large family and a son of the second wife, his prospects were limited. He followed his father's example and moved away to start afresh. He sold his shares in the two town houses (every family member had a share of the assets) but kept majority shares in the dacha and later bought his brothers out. When he had made his own fortune, he built a larger dacha to replace the old version. In 1845, aged twenty-four, armed with his assets of £10,000 (now £1,200,000) and a list of contacts, Philip Jacob set out for Liverpool.

Liverpool shared some similarities with St Petersburg. It was an important port with its own river, the Mersey, but with a more equable climate. It too relied on migrant labour for its wealth, not only the European merchants who flocked there but also the Irish escaping from famine in the 1840s. Unlike its Russian counterpart, it was an ancient city dating back to the 12th century. By the 19th century it had grown rich on the profits of the Atlantic slave trade, although few slaves had actually passed through its port. Goods were shipped to Africa in return for slaves who were transported across the Atlantic to America and the West Indies. On the return journey from America and the West Indies the ships carried sugar, cotton, rum and spices back to Liverpool. Successful slave merchants were often generous donors to local charities (hence their many statues). By the time Philip Jacob arrived in 1845, slave trading by British ships had been outlawed and slavery abolished in 1833, when the British navy patrolled the seas to enforce the ruling. However, illegal trading continued and slavery in America carried on until the end of the American Civil War in 1865. For those who managed to get a ship through the blockade of the South, fortunes could be made. The Civil War was disastrous for Liverpool, making 75% of its textile workers redundant. Before the war, 80% of Britain's raw cotton came from America through Liverpool where it was processed and spun. By 1861 this had fallen to zero. Some was replaced by shipments from India, China and Egypt, where the Pasha had planted cotton. Some still came from America since the Unionists requisitioned the southern cotton and sent it to Northern textile mills or on to Europe. Several Confederate navy ships were built on the Mersey and one of the main suppliers of guns to the South was the London

Armoury Company in London. The merchants, however, adapted quickly, using their existing trade contacts in West Africa to ship commodities like palm oil, which was becoming increasingly important in manufacturing, and trading links were also developed with India and the Far East.

Philip Jacob found work with a firm of commission merchants, where he met the man who would become his best friend, business partner and brother-in-law, Francis Caesar Braun from Bavaria. They moved together into a small house on the sea front where the passing visitors were seagulls and from where they travelled into the city on a horse-drawn omnibus, which went past the door every half hour. Here there were no bears to shoot, only pheasants and rabbits. A year later the two friends made the bold move to set up their own firm, Blessig and Braun, using some of Philip Jacob's capital. The first year made a profit and the prospects seemed good. But the second year brought bankruptcy at a factory abroad that they had supplied with cotton. This was a major setback but they managed to find extra capital from a third partner. For the next three years profits grew from raw cotton and cotton goods, which were exported to Russia, and the import to Liverpool of raw materials like tallow, flax and hemp from Russia. Even in the 19th century these were as important as they had been in the Middle Ages. Other imports were timber, tar and iron, all of which were used for the shipbuilding industry in Britain. Grain became a major import from the 1850s. Liverpool was also well known for its distinctive pottery, creamware, pearlware, delftware and bone china which had a large export market. Much of this went to America. Another export to Russia was locomotives. Blessig and Co were limited in what they could transport since they were small-scale operators with smaller ships. Philip kept regular contact with his family in Russia, taking nephews and cousins to train as clerks. The business continued for six years, after which Philip and Francis became sole owners of Blessig, Braun & Co.

It was time to move out of the city. Philip found a semi-detached house on the sandstone ridge of Edge Hill with three bedrooms, two servants' rooms, a boudoir, dining room, drawing room, kitchen and bathroom. It was a step up, although modest compared to the palace back home. Braun rented a large house in West Derby following his marriage to a girl from St Petersburg. Philip followed suit, marrying Braun's eighteen-year-old sister Carolina, who had joined her brother in Liverpool. Merchants seemed to marry into other mercantile families. They too decamped to West Derby and rented a country house where they lived for ten years and where all of their five children were born. With his healthy fortune Philip Jacob considered retirement. He was now forty. He had worked hard. He could afford it and he had his wife to consider. Carolina had never adapted fully to life in Liverpool. Another concern was the impact of the American Civil War, which would reduce imports of cotton and make life difficult for the company. But Braun wanted to keep going, so Philip Jacob stayed on for another forty years, returning to Russia on holidays to see the family and help fund family interests. Philip had never relinquished his hereditary honorary Russian citizenship and acted for some years as Russian vice-consul in Liverpool, for which he received the Order of St Stanislaus. In 1862, he took the decision to become a British citizen. He was well established in the city, where he had become an important member of the business community and a well-known donor to good causes. He was a director of two large insurance companies and a founding subscriber for the building of the Philharmonic Hall, where he retained a family box. He remained a life-long Conservative and an original member of the Liverpool Conservative Club. Life was good; he had worked hard. But something was lacking. That dacha on the Ligovo road remained imprinted on his memory. Nothing could replace the magic of those wistful summer nights. Some part of his soul had become Russian and he missed the space and simplicity of his Baltic retreat. The next best thing was to build his own Peterhof on English soil. So he bought fifteen acres of fields in West Derby in an area known as Black Moor and sent his architect to Russia to study both the tsarist palace and the dacha. The result was no rustic summer lodge but a more permanent house built in stone with a loggia and decorative wrought-iron arches. Relatively modest in size, it incorporated a mixture of Russian and English styles and a large conservatory, which he filled with exotic plants. There was no need for hot water bottles there. Unfortunately Philip Jacob's good fortune did not extend to his eldest daughter, Emily, who married a German merchant called Louis Frederick Bahr.

It was a fortunate marriage for Louis with Blessig money and connections but an unhappy one for Emily, who was bullied throughout her marriage. At the end of her life, worn out by the abuse, she developed severe depression and ended up in Worthing, cared for by two female companions.

Louis Bahr was a business partner for Schroeders, merchants and brokers in Liverpool. He was part of the migration following George

English Peterhof in West Derby built by Philip Blessig

I, the Hanoverian successor to the English throne. His great uncle Carl Ludwig Bahr had set up a shipping firm in Liverpool called Bahr Behrend in 1835. Unlike Louis, Carl Ludwig (later Charles Louis) had led a colourful life before becoming bankrupt. After studying theology, he fought for Napoleon in Russia before ending up in Liverpool. Many merchants in Liverpool were of German origin. Like the Blessigs and the Thurburns, Louis Bahr was both merchant and consul, in his case German consul and vice-consul for Norway and Sweden. Our grandfather Philip Heinrich Bahr was born in 1881 to Louis and Emily, their only son and the eldest of three children. He looked more like his Hanoverian ancestors than the Alsatian Blessigs. He was large, noisy, exuberant, always working or riding to hounds on a horse large enough to carry him. Family legend has it that he too was bullied and beaten by his father.

Emily Blessig/Bahr in national costume

Despite his wealth, Louis Bahr refused to fund his son's studies at Cambridge, insisting he work in the family firm, so Philip's maternal grandfather Philip Jacob stepped into the breach. He paid for his grandson to sit the natural science tripos at Cambridge, specializing in zoology. As in the case of his father-in-law Patrick Manson, young Philip found that a good knowledge of natural history proved invaluable for tropical medicine where the hosts were animals and birds. At Cambridge he developed into a passionate ornithologist and could have made it his career. But despite his professor Alfred Newton's comment that *"there are many bad doctors in the world, but very few good ornithologists"*, Philip persisted with his medical training and became famous as a tropical specialist. He hadn't planned a career in this field of medicine but was encouraged by his marriage to Patrick Manson's daughter. The first School of Tropical Medicine was not London but Liverpool, which was founded and funded in 1898 by Sir Alfred Lewis Jones. Whether the Blessigs were among the many private donors (including the explorer Mary Kingsley) isn't known.

Philip Jacob sold his beloved Peterhof in 1881, the year of his grandson's birth, and moved to a smaller house in Allerton, where his wife died at the age of forty-six. Unlike his father, he didn't marry again. Nieces and sisters-in-law moved in to look after him. He took up shooting again – he had been a good shot as a young man – renting large estates such as Chirk Castle and Ranton Abbey. Now he spent most of his weekends and holidays with family and friends on the estates, taking over the cottages for his daughters and grandchildren. Although he invested in fine carriage horses, he rode a pony for shooting. He smoked cigars and played whist. A favourite game at the time was known as Raseltin. Its name was derived from the Pasha of Egypt's palace of Ras-el-Tin, where Robert Thurburn had spent so many working hours. Philip still travelled abroad to Germany and St Petersburg. Later in life, when he suffered from Bright's disease, he took the cures at Carlsbad. As a respectable businessman, he thought it only proper to have a family crest. He designed it himself, choosing a griffin holding an axe, a reference to the family's Inn of the Axe, and a worthy motto, "Good repute is better than riches." He had acquired both and retired with honour and a healthy fortune.

Not only did Philip Jacob help our grandfather Philip financially with his studies and give him £10,000 on his marriage (£1,000,000 today), but he also helped many members of the extended family, buying farms in the Baltic provinces for his brother and nephews. He restored the family dacha in Russia and funded the Blessig Institute for the Blind in St Petersburg. He seems a kindly man with a gentle sense of humour. He joked that his only artistic achievement was to list all the firm's bad debts, amounting to thousands of pounds, on the wall of his office under the titles 'Robbers, Half-Wits and Complete Fools.' When he reached eighty he gave up his sporting leases. In 1902, his health began to fail. He died at Beechley in 1904 aged eighty-three after a long and fulfilling life, still very much a European. By the time of his death, the Blessig clan had diminished in numbers. Some had settled on estates in Estonia and Latvia. In 1920 when Estonia became a republic, their estates were appropriated by the Estonian government. In 1939, when Poland was divided between Nazi Germany and Soviet Russia, all the German Balts were transported to Western Poland where the Nazis wanted to create a new German frontier. Many had no connections with Germany other than their names. Families were separated. One female family member took refuge in a convent. Another was interned in a Polish forced labour camp. A cousin was executed by the Gestapo. Some ended up as refugees in the Second World War. One Blessig granddaughter worked for the Americans at Nuremberg. The English descendants fared better. Some fought in the wars. Philip Jacob's grandson Hugh Heyder, whose father was German, was badly wounded on the Somme and was awarded both the Military Cross and the Legion d'Honneur. The last male survivor in England was Edmund Blessig, Philip Jacob's son who suffered badly from asthma. Young Edmund spent his winters abroad with his tutor. His share of his father's fortune meant that he never had to work. He was a generous donor to the London School of Tropical Medicine. As he was not considered bright, it was a surprise to the family when he sold all his Russian railway bonds two years before the revolution. I remember a visit to his home as a child. The wheezing old man with the long fraying beard was almost as terrifying as the huge stuffed bear standing inside the hall holding out a tray for visitors' cards. Uncle Edmund had shot the creature in Canada and brought it home. It looked sad and out of place. We children swore we could see tears trickling from its glass eyes. When

Edmund, the last of the English Blessigs

Edmund died, he left that gloomy house and its eighty acres to our grandfather Philip. It was promptly sold, all its contents going to auction. As for the Villa Blessig, the dacha on the shores of the Gulf of Finland, it was taken over by the Bolsheviks after the revolution as a school for abandoned children.

PACIFIC PARASITES

FIJI 1909–1911

Watercolour by Philip in 1910 of the view from his shack in Suva before the hurricane

After Cambridge, Philip Bahr studied medicine at the London Hospital. One day, while he was examining a patient with an abdominal problem, a young nurse approached him holding out a container with an enormous frothy stool.

"Look how pale and soapy it is. My father taught me these are signs of sprue."

Her father was Sir Patrick Manson. The couple married in 1909 and almost immediately travelled on a two-year expedition to the Fiji Islands to investigate dysentery and filariasis. Travelling with them was William, a young assistant. This research was at Patrick Manson's suggestion and under the auspices of the London School of Tropical Medicine. Manson had suggested that the filariae of the Fiji Islands might relate to new species as yet unknown. At twenty-nine, Philip had completed a diploma in tropical medicine but his experience was limited. Many letters crossed the oceans between him and his father-in-law. Sometimes the replies arrived too late to be useful. It was Philip's first venture into the tropics but Edith had spent her childhood in sub-tropical China.

Philip and Edith left England on the SS *Mooltan* on a grey day in mid-November, weighed down by luggage. Stashed in the hold were three large tin cases and several trunks with books and personal effects, seventeen cases of provisions and household goods, several portmanteaux and two microscopes.

Philip began recording the wildlife as soon as they left port. At Gibraltar he was rewarded with sight of his first eagle. The ship stopped in Marseille to collect the mail. After France, Philip

Engagement photograph of Edith Manson and Philip Bahr

spent most of his time on deck, observing the birds and sketching the coast. They passed the Lipari islands, Stromboli and Naples. Vesuvius was steaming like a pot without a lid. In the narrow straits of Messina where Italy and Sicily almost collide, passengers lined the decks in silence to see the ruins of Messina town. It was early dawn and the only thing visible was the faint pulse of a lighthouse. Mole hills of rubble disguised the ruins. In 1908, during a packed opera festival, an earthquake destroyed the town. A tsunami finished it off; 82,000 died. As the ship steamed slowly by, some of the passengers paused in prayer. Port Said, in contrast, was very much alive and as filthy as Philip expected. Visitors had always been rude about the town, declaring it 'the sewer of migrants' or, more politely, 'a clearing house of nations'. Philip watched the mixed crowd milling on the dock and remarked on the scarred faces of the Sudanese porters, which marked them as ex-slaves. They paid a brief visit to the town in a carriage. On December 1st the SS *Mooltan* passed through the Canal, broad enough, said a surprised Philip, for two battleships to pass each other. The area proved an avian paradise with flamingos, storks, pelicans and marsh harriers all living off the swamps around the salt lakes. Through the Gulf of Suez, keeping Palestine on the left and Africa on the right, the gap widened and the scoured slopes of the Nejaz mountains of Arabia loomed into sight, turning from pink to red as the sun rose. Now there were few signs of bird or human life. It was stifling in the heat. Because of a powerful headwind, the portholes had been screwed down, turning the cabins into saunas. Edith, who was pregnant, suffered greatly. There were soldiers everywhere in Aden (Yemen). The ship stayed only long enough to load and unload the mail. As they entered the Indian Ocean, clouds of flying fish greeted them, weaving and diving over the waves like surfers. The next stop, Ceylon (Sri Lanka), was equally hot but the lush flora and fauna and the brightly coloured butterflies pleased everyone. Buddhist priests in their ochre robes replaced the porters of Port Said. Philip noted the varicose veins in the legs of his rickshaw carrier. On a tour of the Native Hospital he saw his first leper, a case of elephantiasis and a young man suffering from blastomycosis (caused by inhaling fungal spores into the lungs) whose leg had ulcerated down to the bone. Other ubiquitous ailments were dysentery, heat stroke and cirrhosis of the liver. After Sri Lanka, the ship passed the Andaman Islands on December the 12th, after which Philip recorded no stops. He spent his time reading and painting until the ship docked at Freemantle in Australia ten days later. Christmas Day was so hot that they all longed for the hoar frost of an English winter. The ship cruised along the arid Southern Australian coast to Melbourne, where the temperature topped 39°C in the shade. At Sydney, their final destination, they waited five days before the departure of their next boat, the SS *Tofua*, a rolling old coaster, which sent them all to their cabins for the rest of the week until they berthed at Lautoka on the western side of Fiji.

Fiji is one of 330 islands in the Fijian archipelago in the Pacific Ocean to the north of New Zealand and east of Australia. Many are uninhabited. They are volcanic, some with mountains that rise to 1,300 metres, and are covered in tropical forests. Philip's first impressions were not positive. Sugar mills dominated Lautoka and a broken pipe leaked sticky molasses onto the streets. Nor was his first impression of Fijians favourable. His sniggering porters dropped his trunks and cases on the road and ran away in hysterics. From Lautoka, Philip, Edith, William and the luggage took a small boat along the coast to Suva. In fifty-five days of travelling, they had crossed from one side of the world to the other through different climate zones and three oceans. Now they would reach Fiji in twenty-eight hours by plane to New Zealand, including a four-hour journey to Suva.

Even somewhere as remote as the Fiji Islands had suffered from European predators. The islands became attractive to Europeans in the 19th century. Settlers started to grow cotton on tribal land acquired fraudulently. Even veterans of the civil war in America turned up. The missionaries followed. The Fijians put up strong resistance (unlike the Tongans who converted). Later the Fijians converted to Methodism and became very vocal in their beliefs.

Most of the workers in the early cotton fields came from the Solomon Islands and Vanuatu. Many were kidnapped and made to work unpaid. The British government passed an act in 1872 in an attempt to stop the trade. In 1878 indentured labourers were brought from India to work in the sugar cane fields. The Fijians had no need for work. Nor did they want to. Their population had collapsed as a result of white diseases like measles. But they were lucky. A far-seeing governor, Sir Arthur Gordon, made sure that their land and way of life was protected. Today 83% of the land is still owned by Fijians. When Philip and Edith arrived, Fiji had been a Crown colony since 1874.

The first disappointment was that there was no one to meet

them, no one to help transport the bags. Later they found out that Patrick Manson's letter of introduction had travelled with them and that no one of any importance had been notified of their arrival. Another problem was the lack of accommodation. Even the few hotels were full, so they decamped to a fellow doctor's house. Edith, getting heavier with her pregnancy, must have been exhausted. But the networking advantages of a Cambridge education came into play. Philip shared a mutual friend with the government entomologist in Professor Alfred Newton, his professor at Cambridge.

The governor too was a keen ornithologist. The invitations came, including one to Government House. In 1910, Government House was not the colonial mansion we knew later. It was more like a Fijian longhouse with a verandah and attic windows under deep thatched eaves. Chattering mynah birds had invaded the gardens. Imports from India with the Indian sugar cane workers, they did not merit inclusion in Philip's lexicon. As a result of this networking, something came up in the suburb of Tamavua, west of the town. It was not what Philip expected, a shack in the middle of nine humid, mosquito-ridden acres of wilderness, but they had no choice. They set to cleaning and repairing. It was important to make sure it was waterproof since it rained every day in Suva. Philip did much of the work himself, working bare-chested, the sweat pouring down his back until the shack looked like a sharecropper's home in the southern US, minus the rocking chair since the verandah had been converted into a laboratory. When the cart arrived carrying their belongings, they unloaded all the trunks and portmanteaux themselves; the Fijian boys sent to help them took one look and ran away. With gifts from the governor – two domesticated wild chickens and a parrot – it began to look more like home, and there was the promise of fresh eggs. Only when they had finished unpacking, did they sit down on the three chairs they had acquired and, with orange boxes for tables, dine on tinned ham. By February they had settled in and acquired a Fijian cook, Henry, who baked fresh bread every morning. He was less proficient at his stews; no one quite knew what the ingredients were, only that his leftovers managed to kill the cat. Philip worked at the hospital every day. The disorder and lack of organization irked him. The patients wandered around, sleeping anywhere except in a bed. Some lay on the floor on mats or, in the case of the Fijians, underneath their beds. Prisoners slept and worked in chains. The hospital, later replaced by the Colonial War Memorial Hospital in 1923, housed the oldest medical school in the Pacific Islands. The first intake of students were not obvious medical material. After work, which included teaching, Philip retreated to his verandah laboratory with William to pursue his research. Although Philip was young and inexperienced, his research did lead to the discovery of a filarial worm new to Fiji. In true family tradition Philip offered himself up to the mosquitoes. He discovered that the Aedes pseudoscutellaris mosquito transmitted the worm that caused lymphatic filariasis in Fiji – it was an Aedes mosquito peculiar to the Pacific Islands and the worm was called Wucheria Pacifica. Its breeding habits, so crucial to control, eluded him. How was he to know that the mosquito chose to breed in damaged coconut shells high up in the palm canopy?

Lymphatic filariasis causes inflammation of the lymphatic system which, if untreated, leads to elephantiasis, where the arms, legs and other parts blow up like Michelin Man, the same symptoms that Manson had seen in China. Philip also tracked the Shiga housefly as the carrier of the Shigella bacterium. Shigellosis wasn't just a two-day trot to the lavatory. It had serious symptoms and lasted seven days. Philip had no access to libraries and no colleagues in the same field, so he wrote constantly to his father-in-law for advice about the insect vectors he was looking for. Although his degree in zoology helped enormously, he had not studied tropical medicine and these were his first tentative steps. He had to wait five weeks for any reply.

After two months, Philip and Edith embarked on their first visit outside Suva, travelling to the island of Beqa on a government steamer laden with goods for the inhabitants of its leper colony. Accompanying them was the resident medical officer, Dr Prideaux, whose job it was to visit the island once a month. Philip felt sorry for Dr Prideaux, who seemed harassed and overburdened with work. One of thirteen officials and the only white one, he had few helpers and huge responsibilities. The pay was poor and the accommodation sub-standard. Such was the life of a colonial medical officer in 1911. The warden on Beqa and his wife, both Fijians, greeted them formally, the wife crawling submissively on her hands and knees. Philip found himself in a landscape of coral reefs and mountains squashed onto a small island of thirty-six square kilometres. The lepers, many in the advanced stages of the disease, lived together in palm-thatched huts. All had missing fingers and toes. Some were blind. Leprosy is still around today. It is caused by a bacterial infection that affects the nerves, skin, lining of the nose, the upper respiratory tract, limbs and eyes. Like Covid it is transmitted by airborne droplets. Now it is treated with antibiotics. I remember seeing a leper in Nairobi when I was twelve – with a hole where his nose should have been. There was no shortage of patients in Beqa. They came from the whole Pacific area, Indians, Chinese, Samoans, Tongans, Fijians and one lone European, who was thrilled to see a white woman. Beqa is now a tourist resort and famous as the home of firewalkers. It was famous too for its fields of pineapples planted on the slopes behind the village. As Philip and Edith boarded the steamer for the rough crossing back, they were presented with baskets of pineapples but Philip was more excited by the large hawk circling overhead.

On the morning of the 24th of March, back home in Tamavua, Jesse, a medical student from the nearby hostel, came running through the bush to warn Philip of an approaching hurricane. Philip rushed to clear his verandah-lab in preparation for the storm. Hurricanes were fickle and apt to change course at the last moment but every precaution was taken. After all, the house did not look as if it would last five minutes. So everything that could be was lashed down and all the precious equipment moved into the back bedroom. The rain came first, followed by the wind racing at 100 miles an hour. At dusk, as the wind roared, the house was still standing. So they lit the paraffin lamps, making sure they didn't topple over and catch fire. When a pane of glass crashed suddenly to the floor in their bedroom, Edith, who was eight months pregnant, rushed to rescue the microscopes, which had been stored there along with the terrified parrot. They moved the precious microscopes and the parrot into the back bedroom as the rain pummelled on the corrugated iron roof and the shack rocked and swayed. All night the rain fell, flooding the storeroom, forcing them to retreat to the one dry room left, which they shared with clouds of flies and one miserable mongoose. At dawn, the wind dropped, leaving leaves everywhere and the house smelling like a compost heap in autumn. All the butterflies had gone, blown away on the storm, and the great tropical trees lay uprooted. It was, said Philip, "as if some giant bulldozer had flattened them". By some miracle the hospital escaped unscathed and in April, a month after the hurricane, Philip and Edith's daughter was born. Philip described the birds that day in his diary but said little about his new daughter, named Patricia after her grandfather Patrick Manson.

In June the plan was to move to Loma Loma on the island of Bau in the Lau peninsula to carry out further research into filariasis. The Lau islands lay to the north of Fiji between Tonga and Fiji. Bau had been the stronghold of Cakobau, an important Fijian chief in the 19th century. Permission from the current chief, the Buli, had to be obtained first since no one could land without it. Bau was known as an island of cannibals; the sacrificial stone remained in the ground for all to see. In 1833 a French ship, the *Aimable Josephine*, went aground on the reef. Everyone was captured and all the white passengers eaten. The world's most prolific cannibal, according to the *Guinness Book of Records*, was a Fijian called Ratu Udre Udre, who lived on the main island of Viti Levu. Nine hundred stones surrounded his grave, each one representing someone he had consumed.

The family left the Tamavua shack on a wet morning in June, Edith carrying her new baby. Philip didn't like the look of the horse that was dragged up the hill to carry their possessions, all skin and bones and with an evil eye. Perhaps the horse took exception to his passengers for when the cases and the two microscopes had been loaded into the carriage, it decided to bolt all the way back to Suva town, galloping down the steep hills and narrow bends. The Indian driver leapt into a ditch, followed by the microscopes. It was an inauspicious beginning to Philip's discovery of the outer islands. Once the luggage was rescued they tried again with a more agreeable beast. First they took a boat to Levuka, an island with a buccaneering past. It had been the capital in 1874 after Fiji became a British Crown Colony. But in 1882 the government moved to Suva. In 1911 it was still prosperous, full of German and Danish merchants and enterprising Samoans. Philip comments about Pacific Island women in his diary were rarely complimentary. When a huge whale-like Samoan spread her blubber over a bench next to him on the boat, he noted his revulsion in his diary. Other passengers were more to his taste, like the English Beddoes family who lived in a remote lighthouse north of Vanua Levu, the second largest island in the Fijian group. Like most lighthouses, Wailagi Lala was prefabricated in Britain, and shipped out to Fiji, where it was assembled and placed on its coral atoll, all of seventy-five acres and only three metres above sea level. The lighthouse was visited once every three months, otherwise the family were left alone. It was extraordinary how many Europeans were living and working on the island of Vanua Levu. There was the wealthy German planter called Jennings with his copra plantation. Copra, oil extracted from dried coconut kernels, was the most profitable crop in the islands and many planters like Jennings became very rich. Jennings had come from Bremen in 1860 and married the chief's daughter. On the chief's death, the locals invited him to be their ruler. Jennings saw an opportunity for German influence, so he returned home and begged an interview with Bismarck. Bismarck showed no interest, so the flag that flew over Vanua Levu remained solidly British. Jennings invited Philip to dinner, desperate to speak his native tongue and share his good German wine (few British spoke German like Philip). Seventy-two-year-old Jennings was a cultured man, a lover of music and good conversation, an improvement, said Philip, on the British. Another planter in Vanua Levu, a rich Chinaman, fell victim to Philip's prejudices. He didn't share his father-in-law's admiration of the Chinese and wrote of "the yellow peril getting everywhere". The wealthier inhabitants of the island were Tongans who, to Philip's European eyes, seemed organized and disciplined and lived in well-built houses with nice furniture. Philip considered the Fijians more happy-go-lucky. Fijian houses known as bures were built to keep out the sun. They had a single door and the odd window, were made of wood and dried straw bound together by rope. A deep roof made of leaves hung over the door like a tea cosy. The largest house, the Valé, was for the women and children. Coconut-leaf mats covered the packed-earth floors. The women cooked in earth pits in a corner, coughing and blinking in the thick smoke. Equally smoky were the houses where male clan members met to chat.

Loma Loma, where Philip and Edith were to spend the next nine months, was one of the islands in the Bau archipelago. It was volcanic, with waterfalls and hot springs, white beaches and coral reefs. The family took Henry their cook and Jesse the medical student. A comfortable mosquito-proofed house awaited them. But food was scarce and they had to live on tinned food. The village was home to the local chief, the Buli, who lined up with the other villagers to meet this 'famous doctor from London' who wanted

Fijian bure
Alamy stock photo

to take their blood. There was a strict etiquette to queuing – you queued up according to rank, with women and girls last. Philip was looking for the epitrochlear lymph nodes (swollen glands in their upper arms), a symptom of filariasis. The chief said they called this disease waganga and the worms, manu manus. Philip had his eye on a Tongan with impressively enlarged glands, hoping to remove some for testing. But the Tongan would have none of it. Eventually bullied by the chief, he gave in and Philip removed the filariae (the manu manus) from the man's arm, placing them under his microscope to show the village. Everyone came running. The young girls took a quick look and screamed, "It's a snake, a snake!" After this, gaggles of young women followed Philip around, giggling behind his back. Loma Loma was known for its surplus of young single women and for its busy divorce rate. At least in 1911 divorcing wives weren't hunted down and eaten. One wife in the 19th century had to sit while her husband ate her arm bit by bit. She converted to Christianity just before she died.

Apart from Fijians, Tongans and Samoans, there was a diverse population of outsiders, people with a history who had found their way to this remote island. Philip found another German called Fischer abandoned in his hut. Knowing that he was dying, Fischer begged to speak German with Philip. For their part the locals tolerated the odd behaviour of this young Englishman who spent his time looking at manu manus. They followed Philip when he went to trap mosquitoes in his cages and crowded round when he netted flies for his collections. They observed his passion for birds and watched him sketch scenes that took his fancy. They screamed when he showed them a parasitic worm wriggling on a bed of salt. They did, however, expect him to attend church on Sundays. Philip called the service "the pantomime", although the singing was remarkable, but the flirting of the young girls left much to be desired, although he did concede that some were attractive. One woman always arrived late, making a graceful entrance down the aisle. Her father, a chief, had left her an income of £500 a year. Everyone wondered how she managed to spend that in Loma Loma.

Henry the cook must have tried Edith's patience. As well as his mediocre cooking, Henry kept irregular hours. Sometimes he would disappear for days, "gone to see my grandmother", was his excuse. One day his relations turned up outside the house with their begging bowls to share Henry's savings. Henry was in a quandary. The disadvantages of a large extended family now outweighed the advantages. He hid his gains underneath his mattress and started pillaging the store cupboard. When the roof began to leak, Henry sheepishly owned up. He had sold the tin roof panels. Edith must have forgiven him, for he stayed. Servants were not easy to find on Loma Loma and Edith was often alone.

Kava ceremony
Alamy stock photo

One important social event that Philip could not avoid was the kava ceremony since he was the guest of honour. The kava drink was made from the root of a plant from the deadly nightshade family, which was chewed and spat into a communal bowl. It was a narcotic and a sedative, which numbed the mouth and lips of its imbibers. In Loma Loma the event was a proper affair, conducted by a master of ceremonies, with singing and dancing and acrobatic stunts, the smell of native cigarettes wrapped in banana leaves mingling with the sweat of the performers. Philip woke the next morning with a headache, dry mouth and terrible diarrhoea. The taste, he said, was "bitter, peppery and nauseating".

By mid-December it was time to leave the island. William went on ahead. Henry, poorer for his relations' avarice, and Jesse, the medical student who had spent his nights partying, sailed back to

Suva with them. Edith was pregnant again, so they decided to break the journey in Taveuni, an island off the coast of Viti Levu, known as the Garden Island. A shield volcano with fertile soil and plentiful rain, it was home to large coconut plantations and more than one millionaire. Before checking in to the hotel, Philip and Edith happened to run into the Taite family, owners of the largest coconut plantation in Taveuni, who had made their fortune in the goldfields of Australia. An invitation to stay followed. For Philip and Edith, it was a chance to luxuriate in a bath (there were none in the house in Loma Loma or the shack in Suva) and enjoy the modern sanitary arrangements. After a few days of civilized living, it was a shock to return to Tamavua, where they found their nine acres overrun with wild dogs. Still, work had to continue. The instruments and cages of mosquitoes were returned to the verandah laboratory. Visits to the hospital resumed. Then a plea came from a desperate Dr Prideaux on one of the far islands. Would Philip travel to Sigatoka where his wife was seriously ill with typhoid? There was no one else who could go. It would be a difficult journey with nowhere to stay other than villages that would not always be welcoming and it would rain every day. Philip thought of the rare birds he might see in the forests, the thrill of travelling wild and the research he might do. He picked up two nurses from the hospital and took a small boat up the coast from where he disembarked at a leper station. Now they had a journey inland of sixty miles but it could have been 160, the pace was so slow. The policeman and Indian guide who accompanied them with a mule and four skeletal horses were little help. There were no trails; the interior of the island was an obstacle race of eroded volcanic ridges corrugated by gullies. Philip and the nurses walked most of the way leading the horses. On the first day they crossed through sugar cane fields owned by the Fiji Vancouver Sugar company. Every day the rain unleashed clouds of ravenous mosquitoes. Now and then ghostly apparitions would emerge from the forest, like the toothless white man who led them to a hut full of similarly etiolated men drinking whisky and tea. Philip took one look and escaped into the forests that covered the mountains. This was bird paradise. Philip was in his element. The villages, however, were uninviting. You never knew what kind of welcome to expect and would you get something to eat? Sometimes there was tea, sometimes tea and biscuits, sometimes pineapples but more often nothing. It was normal to sleep in wet clothes. In one hut, a pile of rags in the corner metamorphosed into a man. The chief was indifferent. "He's dying." This lack of care for the disabled and elderly was all too common despite the benefits of tribal living. In the next village, there were no dying elders, just a terrible stench that hung in the air. As Philip and the nurses rode out the next morning, they found a cemetery with half-buried bodies. In the next village, the chief boasted touches of civilization with his decanters and glasses but they were only for show. Tea, biscuits and coconut milk was their last meal before they dropped down to the banana plantations of Sigatoka, where they found a wretched Mrs Prideaux alone in her house. Passing Indian traders had brought typhoid to the town and she had caught it from her lodger. His corpse lay for fifteen days in the heat until a coffin could be found. Philip was shocked; the house was not fit for humans, let alone colonial officials like Dr Prideaux. The hospital didn't take white patients, so the two nurses volunteered to stay behind.

Philip returned to Suva by boat to face the threat of another hurricane as the family were preparing to leave Fiji. They put their portmanteaux against the windows and doors and all the baggage accumulated during their stays, such as caged birds and animal skins. The wind abated the next day. There was two weeks' grace before loading a cart and riding down to the port to board the Moana. On the day of departure as the ship readied to sail, Henry and Jesse, dressed in Philip's handouts, stood on the dock, hands clasped, heads bowed as if in mourning. No one sang a Loma Loma farewell for Philip and Edith. They left Fiji as they had arrived, in a thick mist. They were on their way to America via Honolulu. It would be several months before they reached England on the *Lusitania*, the most luxurious ship afloat, a contrast to the hardships of Fiji. They just made it home in time for my father, Clinton, to be born on May 5th 1911. Philip's assistant William made his own way home. What he thought of the trip is not recorded but he stayed with Philip all his life and became a loyal and very competent technician and friend. Philip wrote a 192-page report on filariasis and elephantiasis in Fiji and illustrated it with his own paintings, drawings and photographs. These illustrations were drawn to scale with the aid of a camera lucida (the subjects were minute) and are exquisitely detailed works of art now in the Wellcome Collection.

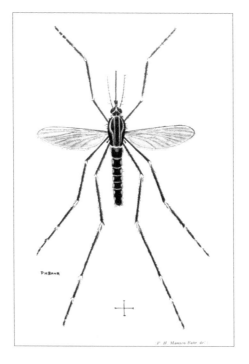

Drawing of mosquito by Philip
The Wellcome Collection London

DYSENTERY AND WAR

EGYPT 1915–1920

Captain Philip Bahr with his unit in 1914. Philip bottom right

Philip had no time to enjoy home life. A year after his return from Fiji, he was sent to Ceylon (Sri Lanka) to investigate the causes of tropical sprue. Sprue caused ulceration of the mouth and chronic inflammation of the small intestine and was thought to be a bacterial infection. Philip cycled miles around the island with his medical equipment balanced on his bike and proved the medical fraternity wrong. It was, he announced confidently, caused by a pathogenic yeast. In 1915, now a captain in the Royal Army Medical Corps, he found himself in Gallipoli with the tool of his trade: his microscope, and the challenging task of reducing the scale of disease among the troops. It was dangerous work even for doctors. Philip's experience of working in difficult conditions like Fiji would have helped, although he had gone from one extreme of climate to another.

The Gallipoli campaign lasted eleven months, with 250,000 casualties on both sides and 90,000 British soldiers evacuated because of illness. Some of these were diseases Philip had seen in Fiji, such as cholera, typhoid and dysentery, and were the same as had plagued the Pasha's Egypt. These were biblical scourges in a land of scourges. Dysentery rendered a soldier useless. This was not just a day or two of the runs. It was chronic and affected most of the men. With few washing facilities they couldn't clean themselves and they suffered in stained and stinking clothes. This added to the other noxious smells: the rotting corpses that couldn't be retrieved under heavy gun fire and the open latrines. In summer the heat was extreme. The winter brought frostbite and the loss of fingers and toes. Sir Ronald Ross, Patrick Manson's protégée, was sent to deal with the malaria problem. Patrick had volunteered, but at sixty-nine and in poor health, it wasn't an option. The campaign ended in defeat for the British. Nothing had been achieved other than a better understanding of some of the diseases for the next stage of the war provoked by the Turkish attack on the Suez Canal in 1915.

Philip spent the next two years in Cairo as a pathologist at two military hospitals and one for prisoners of war. It was a very different Egypt from Robert Thurburn's time. Philip would have met the large tribe of Thurburns from Scotland, Argentina and Egypt who had attended his wedding in London. Britain had occupied Egypt and the Sudan since 1882. It was supposed to be temporary but lasted until the 1950s. At the beginning of the war, when the Turks allied themselves to the Germans and Austrians, Britain declared Egypt a protectorate and deposed the Khedive Abbas, grandson of Muhammad Ali. Egypt became the front line in the war when the Ottomans crossed the Sinai Peninsula to take the Suez Canal.

The logistical problems of the Sinai campaign were enormous, water and disease being major challenges faced by General Allenby. His Expeditionary Force included 50,000 troops from two infantry divisions, cavalry units and soldiers from the Empire, including India, New Zealand and Australia. Few of the Indian troops could speak English and only one or two of their officers spoke Hindi. A unit of Gurkhas and some French made up the total. Allenby also acquired T.E. Lawrence as his personal liaison officer.

This influx of foreign troops into Egypt infuriated the locals, not least the behaviour of the Anzacs who tended to get into alcohol-fuelled fights. There was a boom in prostitution and sexually transmitted disease. British conscription of 500,000 Egyptians for the Labour and Camel Transport Corps didn't go down well either. The Camel Corps had a vital role in ferrying water, food and medical supplies to the front and received little recognition at the end of the war. The requisitioning of buildings and animals and the buying up of food stocks alienated the locals further. Allenby insisted on proper medical facilities for his troops, as had the Pasha in his day. During the desert campaign men were more at risk from disease than war. Apart from the more deadly diseases such as malaria, cholera and dysentery, there were the minor ailments that could turn septic: boils and typhus, insect bites, cuts or sunburn. Gonorrhoea was always present. Thirst was normal. Allowed only one water bottle a day during marches in intense heat, some men drank their urine. Even that was scarce. Water was a constant problem for both horses and men. Sometimes the horses went days without. The men got used to water dug from local wells tasting of sand and chlorine. There were constant irritations like lice and bed bugs. Inventive soldiers hung their clothes over ant hills and waited for the ants to emerge and eat the lice and the eggs. As for the plagues of flies there was little the men could do other than make sure that all manure and human faeces were carried away to reduce the flies and the rats. Dead animals were burnt. Unlike the war in Europe, the men were inactive much of the time. They felt guilty that their fellow countrymen were dying on the Western Front. For them it was a waiting game, sitting in tents sweating in the heat, bored by the monotonous terrain of sand and dunes inhabited by snakes and scorpions and giant rats. When the khamsin blew, it whipped the dust into a roiling whirlwind, which penetrated clothes, eyes, food and drinking water. While the wind lasted, and it could be several days, the temperature rose over forty degrees but at least it got rid of the flies.

In 1917 Philip was transferred to Palestine where he was put in charge of field laboratories. During his time there he dealt with a serious cholera outbreak, which had started among troops in a transit camp in Sinai. First he had to trace the source by examining mountains of excrement. He sent for 'stools' to inspect – stools in our family were never things you sat on. These 'stools' came in buckets with a caravan of camels, twenty-five of them travelling

Philip outside his field laboratory

from Beersheba five days from camp in temperatures of forty degrees. Every bucket had to be examined immediately before being returned to Beersheba on the backs of the same camels. But a major problem for the army was malaria, especially in the Jordan Valley, where both Allenby's army and the Turks suffered big losses. One day while Philip was out sketching in the desert, he came face to face with the general. They discovered a shared passion for ornithology. The bird talk quickly changed to medicine when Allenby discovered that the young captain was the principal malaria specialist in his medical unit. Could Dr Bahr save his men from dying before the next advance? Philip saw an opportunity. He had long been trying to obtain small mobile malaria diagnosis stations for rapid diagnosis. These mobile stations had to be dismantled and moved on the backs of the long-suffering camels from camp to camp. There were five different kinds of malaria. Some were more fatal than others. It was essential to know which kind you were treating. Allenby told Philip he could have anything he asked for. He got six mobile units.

His was No. 3 Field Laboratory. A handwritten sign in pencil on the left flap read, "specimens to be left here". It took six weeks to train the field workers. Doctors, including Philip, worked in shifts sixteen hours a day in the heat, examining 40,000 blood slides. They discovered that the type of malaria in Palestine was a virulent strain of Plasmodium falciparum, which affected the areas to which the Egyptian Expeditionary Force were heading.

In October 1917 the Egyptian Expeditionary Force marched up the coast and, with the aid of planes and bombs, captured Beersheba, home of the smelly 'stools'. Allenby moved on to Jaffa and from there to Jerusalem, which the army entered in December 1917. Unlike the Kaiser, who rode in twenty years earlier, Allenby entered the city on foot, to the cheers of a weary population who lined the streets and even climbed onto the Jaffa Gate for a better view. He had delivered Jerusalem "as a Christmas present for the British Nation", as Lloyd George had requested. Allenby moved quickly to protect the religious sites, putting his Indian Muslim soldiers to guard the mosques. The doctors, including Philip, found themselves dealing with crowded hospitals full of the starving and dying. After braving the flies and the stench in the Jewish Hospital, they discovered wards full of German and Turkish soldiers suffering from pellagra, a serious disease caused by malnutrition. There was malaria too, for despite the lack of open water, Jerusalem's mosquitoes had adapted to breed in the rain-water cisterns, of which there were many, turning the city into a reservoir of the disease. In February 1918 Allenby captured Jericho and established a new front line from the Mediterranean to the Dead Sea.

Philip's diary starts in February 1918 with one word, "rain". He was in Jaffa microscoping bloods from the local people, looking for malarial parasites. The rain watered the orange groves and refreshed the fields of crowsfoot grass and purple irises on the way to Jericho.

His work kept him on the move, visiting hospitals and giving lectures. This was pleasanter than examining buckets of faeces and it introduced him to the cultural and archaeological sites of Palestine. He often slept in the local hospital. Most were run by religious orders. In one run by the French Sisters of Charity, he camped in the operating theatre as all the beds were full. His temporary residence in Jerusalem was the German Augusta Victoria Hospital on the Mount of Olives set in a garden of trees. It was founded in 1910 as a guest house for German pilgrims. In its magnificent tiled chapel were mosaics of the Kaiser and his wife Augusta Victoria. Today the hospital provides special care for Palestinians from the West Bank and Gaza. Philip's German would have come in useful again, although being too obviously German was inadvisable.

The peace of this haven was broken only by a masked shrike singing in the olive trees. Philip lay awake listening. From his base here, he built in visits to the ancient sites like Lachish, which he described as piles of rubble. But the countryside was a pleasant surprise. He observed it with the eye of the artist as he rode through on horseback, enjoying the pastoral settings and the wadis with their clear water. He visited camps, clearing stations, nurses' bases, military headquarters and clinics, spending his nights away from Jerusalem. This required travel usually on horseback but sometimes he was taken by a Red Cross car. The main problem was the state of the roads, not an ambush by Turks. If time allowed, he would stop and sketch, or have a swim in a wadi. In one hospital he discovered a case of leishmaniasis, transmitted by the bite of a sandfly, which he recorded in his diary, filling the rest of the page with bird sightings. He accompanied the French Mission to the Jewish quarter in Jerusalem, where there were rumours of Turkish and German spies in the convents. There were lunches and dinners with friends, sometimes in hotels. It doesn't sound much like war, although the work he did was crucial.

On May 20th the order came to move. Philip joined a motor convoy

Rural scenes of Palestine, 1915

back to Jerusalem. Two days later he moved to the headquarters of the Desert Corps near Wadi Qelt in the Jordan Valley.

This was the worst time and place to camp when the temperatures ranged from 21 to 40°C and the area was notorious for malaria. Allenby had chosen the site for its strategic importance, for its distance from the Hedjaz railway, which posed a serious Turkish threat to the British, and for its plentiful streams with good water for washing and drinking. The surrounding area was a Garden of Eden, with trees and sites like the monastery of Mar Saba, hanging from a cliff pock-marked with hermits' caves. The long narrow Jordan Valley was deeply etched into the land 200 metres below sea level. Sheer cliffs on both sides rose to 1,700 metres. Allenby, who had already lost men to malaria – none of the men and few of the cavalry had mosquito nets, asked Philip what he should do. Philip advised a move to higher ground. It helped, as did the clearing of canals and the draining of the marshes and swamps. Philip often rose at dawn, the coolest time of day, to walk in the hills behind camp to sketch and observe the hopeful vultures perched on the bluffs above the river. His letters home were illustrated with amusing cameos of Sinai. Sometimes he would go for a swim and find himself sharing the pools with local Arabs. One day, despite the heat, he walked five miles to Mar Saba monastery, returned home, saddled his horse and rode another one and a half hours to the Dead Sea for a swim, galloping back in time for dinner.

Meanwhile, the soldiers in the camps were doing their best to reduce the malaria risk. They cut down any greenery and poured oil on stagnant pools to prevent the laying of eggs. There were still the usual niggles like scorpions, snakes and jackals that howled at night. The white salt dust that blew off the Dead Sea stuck to clothes and hair and infiltrated the drinking water. Bully beef boiled in its tins. The death rate for horses rose to over 600 a week and all the corpses had to be removed and burned. The malaria and influenza toll increased daily (the Spanish flu had reached Palestine). The only treatment for malaria was quinine. Even the sturdy camels died from Surra fever, a disease spread by horse flies. Allenby's army was heavily outnumbered by Turkish and German troops in trenches higher up in the Judaean hills, so he resorted to deceit. Dummy horses covered in blankets were assembled to fill the gaps left by the dead animals while the living ran around in circles creating clouds of dust suggesting the presence of a large army. Extra fires at night added to the deception. This didn't prevent the frequent attacks or German strafing. In July, Philip recorded shelling and five casualties. It didn't stop him travelling to give his lectures. Sometimes he returned on the night train and once he stopped off to go to the races!

In August, Philip's leave came up. A sea plane took him to Taranto in Italy. From there he boarded a troop train up the coast, sharing a carriage with an Italian doctor. It was a long, slow journey with innumerable halts. He noticed beggars everywhere and a lack of able-bodied men. The workers in the fields he passed were women and elderly men. Women had even replaced the porters at the railway stations. But there were stops for swimming and the military camps provided accommodation. He reached Toulon on the 7th of August. At Cherbourg, after a medical inspection, he took a bath and lunched in a hotel. Cherbourg, he wrote in his diary, was packed with French destroyers and sea planes and he had to wait for his ship to leave. Five weeks later Philip was on his way back to Sinai when his ship was attacked by two torpedoes off the Italian coast. No one was hurt and he still made it in time for the great offensive in Palestine. On his drive to camp in the Red Cross car convoy, he passed a bombed German field hospital. At the next railhead, littered by German lorries, they found dead horses and three Turkish corpses reeking of dysentery. At the end of September the army moved to take Damascus. There they found 10,000 prisoners in a terrible state, who had to be transported to the railway and taken to Egypt for treatment. Peace came with the Kaiser's abdication on Sunday the 10th of November, after the Turks had sued for peace and Austria capitulated. Philip wrote in his diary, "RED LETTER DAY!" He celebrated the armistice of the 11th with fireworks, whisky and champagne in the desert town of Lodd. It fell to Allenby to tell Prince Feisal, his ally, that he would not have Syria as promised, despite his work with Lawrence to help the allies. The Arabs had been misled. Feisal was not told that Mr Sykes and Monsieur Picot had already divided Palestine among themselves in 1916. The French got Syria. The British got Palestine. Two years later, Feisal was given Iraq by the British. The defeat resulted in the break-up of the Ottoman Empire, which the British had opposed so fiercely in Robert Thurburn's time. It led to the formation of new countries: Lebanon, Jordan and Syria. It led also to a token independence for Egypt but the costs had been huge. For Philip the war had been productive. He had gained valuable medical experience, which helped him in his examination for membership of the Royal College of Physicians, where his first question was on dysentery! He was returning home with a full sketch book, including a watercolour of a rectal ulcer caused by amoebic dysentery and a drawing of a colonic ulcer biopsy, both of which appeared as illustrations in his book on *The Diagnosis and Treatment of Dysentery and Diarrhoea*. Later he was awarded the DSO for his work – perhaps all those buckets of stinking faeces he examined were worth it.

AFRICA AND THE HOME COUNTRY

1911–1948

Captain Knight with his golden eagle Mr Ramshaw

My father, Philip Edmund Clinton, known as Clinton, was born two days after his parents' return from Fiji. The most visible clue to his German ancestry was his large head. The rest of him looked Levantine (and he was sometimes mistaken as such), with his swarthy skin, dark hair and eyes. Although he shared his father's build, booming voice and boisterous enthusiasm, in temperament he was more like his grandfather Patrick Manson, who died when he was eleven, sharing his passion for research, the natural world and hunting. He saw no contradiction in this. Shooting was a tribal hunt with friends who shared their knowledge over a boozy meal. Sometimes it meant hours standing in icy marshes at dawn waiting for the ducks to fly over and almost cost him his life when he was dragged under by his waders in the Romney Marsh. When help finally arrived, Clinton's heart had stopped. It was in all the papers, "Duck-shooting doctor escapes death."

Clinton was one of five children: two boys and three girls. At eight he was sent to a Dickensian prep school, followed by public school where he filled his time with work and sport. His letters home are not personal; they politely ask for stamps and pocket money and sometimes list sporting success. You would never guess that he was bullied for being "that German boy" (he was seven in 1918). Soon after this, Philip dropped the umlaut and changed his name to Manson-Bahr. It rolled well off the tongue and helped promote Philip in the medical world. Despite the bullying, Clinton's reports show a clever, hard-working boy who achieved good results.

The main family home was a tall house in Weymouth Street in

London. Like Patrick Manson's house nearby, the ground floor was taken up by Philip's private consulting rooms. The grandmothers on both sides lived nearby and came for tea and whist. Henrietta Isabella Manson smoked like a chimney while poor sad Emily Bahr sat demurely in a corner, grateful for the company. Edith my grandmother, now the matriarch of the family, took responsibility for her sisters, one of whom was left a penniless widow in South Africa with five children and was brought home to live with the family in Wimpole Street. The Blessig and Bahr money funded a comfortable life, with two homes and annual skiing trips to Lenk paid for by Uncle Edmund Blessig who took over a whole hotel for three weeks.

Clinton felt most at home at the country cottage in Kent, roaming the countryside with his brother collecting birds' eggs (only one from each nest) and adding them to their collection in the room above the garage. He rode to hounds and in the steeplechases for the local point to point. He shared a love of ornithology with his father and brother. After school he went to Trinity College, Cambridge, where he studied medicine and where, it is said, his brother Hugh kept a falcon tethered on a post in the quad. Like his father and brother, he did his medical training at the London Hospital and after graduating won a coveted Fulbright Scholarship at the Mayo Clinic in Minnesota. When asked about his time there, all he said was that the duck shooting was marvellous. Back home, he passed his membership exams at the young age of twenty-seven. He got into his red MG, a gift from his mother, and raced home to Kent, bumping down Titsey Hill to tell his family of his success. Philip ignored him but Edith was thrilled. Perhaps this disappointing reaction from his father convinced him to sign up for the Colonial Service and disappear to Tanganyika (Tanzania) in 1939 just after he had passed his diploma in tropical medicine and hygiene.

Clinton was an ideal candidate for the Colonial Service, which drew its personnel from an elite group of highly educated people.

Interviews and examinations were tough. Officially the exams were open to anyone, but in reality, white British were preferred, although the occasional Indian, some Europeans and even the odd woman slipped through. The qualities required were those of the public school: leadership, patriotism, conservatism, sportsmanship, a sense of fairness, good manners and respect for British traditions. Although Clinton was a product of his time and upbringing, he had begun to move away from the strictures of his class. At work, he noticed how many young children languished in the TB wards at the London Hospital and how most lacked shoes. The Colonial Service suited him perfectly. It was full of like-minded souls with their own reasons for escape. The Colonial Service relied on Scottish and Irish doctors to fill its posts. There were many of them, and as in Patrick Manson's day, they suffered discrimination when applying for posts at home. Most applicants preferred to go east in Africa, where the climate was kind and where they had a better chance of surviving to pensionable age. West Africa was too disease-ridden, although the term of service was shorter and there was the incentive of an early pension, if you lived long enough. Among the advice given to aspiring colonial officers was 'to join the club'. Being clubbable and a 'good chap' added to your appeal. Clinton passed the exams and was sent to Tanganyika (Tanzania) in 1939, travelling on a crowded troopship. Then, the East African coastal forest stretched from Mozambique to Somalia. In 1975, when Clinton returned on a World Health project, most of the forest had gone, burnt for charcoal.

The colonial officers I met as a child were committed to their work. They often spoke one or more of the native languages. They cared about the people they served. They covered many areas, medical and veterinary services, schools, infrastructure, water supplies, forestry and agriculture. They were responsible for law and order, local courts and district councils. They had good relations with the local chiefs and took their complaints seriously. People back home in England sneered at us colonials for living the good life and exploiting 'the natives'. I found this when I went to boarding school at twelve. But life wasn't always good. It wasn't romantic like *The Flame Trees of Thika*. It was lonely; often the wives couldn't take the isolation – there were no clubs in the bush and sometimes no other white women – and there was always the threat of disease and the lure of the bottle. Even the romantic roars of lions at night couldn't mitigate the boredom. Doris Lessing's *The Grass is Singing* describes the other side. The heroine, a young white woman driven mad by loneliness and heat, commits the unpardonable sin of sex with an African servant. Clinton, however, was never bored. The wilder the bush, the more he loved it. Colonial officers didn't have a stake in the land, they didn't own farms, they lived on meagre salaries. Their investment was emotional not financial. In many countries they were (and still are) much respected. Some stayed on in Kenya after independence to help set up administrative systems for the new governments. Although many in Kenya were concerned that independence was rushed and unprepared, they accepted the wish of the Africans to run their own countries.

When war broke out in Ethiopia in 1940, Clinton joined the Royal Army Medical Corps as a lieutenant-colonel and moved north to Kenya. This was a happy time. The huge empty spaces of Northern Kenya and Ethiopia remained close to his heart all his life. Whenever he could, he disappeared to the Simien Mountains to film the rare Ethiopian Oryx for his cine collection. This volcanic plateau, rising 4,000ft above the plains, was Clinton's sort of place, remote and dangerous and home to many species of animals and birds. The closest he got to a primate were the noisy Gelada monkeys that gathered on the plateau to dig for grubs. Clinton was not alone; he had a guide and porters. He liked roughing it, living on tins and biltong. He managed one frame of an oryx's backside in the distance before it was time to return. On the way back to Addis Ababa, a

Clinton in the King's African Rifles, Kenya, 1940

chieftain leapt out into the road and flung open his cape, exposing his raddled parts. Clinton pronounced it the worse goddam case of gonorrhoea he had ever seen. He dug into his rucksack and produced some penicillin. The ras grinned, waved his arms expansively and pointed to a herd of cattle.

"Shoot!"

Clinton duly shot his supper, at which point a crowd of angry villagers pursued him demanding payment. This was the kind of life he enjoyed.

The Italians had occupied Ethiopia, Eritrea and part of Somalia since 1935. But the war with Kenya began with an Italian air raid in 1940 on a local base after Mussolini had declared war on Britain and France. The King's African Rifles were rushed to the border. They were heavily outnumbered by the Italians based in Ethiopia. The Africans had been in no hurry to sign up. Perhaps they remembered the huge loss of life of the native soldiers and porters from both the German and British sides in East Africa in the First World War. But the drought and famine that struck in 1940, 'the famine of the Italian' the Africans called it, resulted in a surge of recruits who saw the army as a way out; 30% of the Kings' African Rifles were African and yet no African could rise above the rank of warrant officer. The war lasted barely a year. The Italians failed to put up much of a fight. Clinton travelled north to set up medical facilities for the occupying colonial troops in Ethiopia. He sat in the truck at the front of the convoy, his gun at the ready to shoot the dinner. One of Clinton's tasks in Addis Ababa included the setting up of an approved brothel for the South African troops based there. The women had to be examined and passed clear of disease. One of Clinton's favourite lines at parties was, "Well, you know there wasn't a clean woman in the whole of Addis Ababa?" It never failed to shock.

Clinton met our mother, Joan, at a party during the war. In different circumstances, they might never have met. Joan had turned up in Kenya by chance and liked it so much she stayed. Kenya was full of eligible officers. Single women were in the minority. Clinton and Joan married in January 1943, after which Clinton spent time travelling between Kenya and Ethiopia, leaving Joan with friends. But the end of the war brought the end of Clinton's service in the army. He returned to England jobless, with a wife and two small children whom the family had yet to meet. The ship was crammed with families from the African colonies. In our luggage we carried tins of sardines to eat on the voyage, canned butter and ham for the family in England and Clinton's booty from Ethiopia, a Mauser rifle and an expensive Zeiss microscope. Clinton's reluctance to return to the 'home' country was probably shared by most of the passengers on board. When we docked at Tilbury, Joan peered over the railings at the sepia crowd gathered below.

"They look so shabby."

"There's been a war," said Clinton curtly.

Returning to England was a dismal prospect for him. He was in no rush to return home. And yet it was the sort of home that most people would have been reluctant to leave for the rough edges of Africa. He felt a sense of failure. Now he had to settle for the country cottage in Pootings in Kent, where the family had taken refuge during the war. It was not what he wanted. He didn't get on well with his father. Although our grandfather Philip was no loving grandfather to us, he had many admirers and his students adored him. They queued for his lectures, delivered at full volume without notes and laced with witty anecdotes. He was a busy man. He collected awards and honours like we collected stamps. He travelled, wrote books and edited the bible of tropical medicine, *Manson's Tropical Diseases*, for thirty-nine years. He was director of the London School of Hygiene and Tropical Medicine for ten years and consultant physician to the Colonial Office for twenty. He also ran a lucrative private practice from Harley Street. By the time we came home, Philip had been knighted for services to tropical medicine and was now Sir Philip Manson-Bahr. This honour came in the same year as his younger son Hugh's death. Hugh had followed his brother and father studying medicine at the London Hospital. When still a student during the Second World War, strangers in the street would thrust white feathers in his face. Even friends of the family with sons at the front asked why he wasn't out there fighting. Hugh had tried to sign up, but Philip thought he would be more use as a qualified doctor. Hugh graduated only to find that Philip had arranged a medical officer's post for him in Kenya. The voyage out in 1941 was traumatic. As the ships sailed up the East African coast, German submarines circled like sharks. One ship went down. Hugh could only watch as women and children drowned while his ship steamed on. This had a profound effect on him, as did his posting in Kitale a small town in the Rift Valley, about 350 kilometres from Nairobi. The only other white person was a middle-aged English matron. Hugh was twenty-five years old. He hated the loneliness. He hated the heat and the dust. He missed his home, his dogs and his friends. Unlike his brother Clinton, there was nothing in Kenya that appealed to him and he was far from any social life. The matron found him dead in his room. It was suicide. The family pronounced him a casualty of war. His letters home spoke of his despair. Clinton was sent to identify the body. He never spoke about it.

The tragedy aged my grandmother Edith. She had done all she could to support the war effort, hosting cockney children from London in the rooms above the stables. But the cockneys found the silence and the meals of vegetables unbearable and returned to the bombs of London. She had filled the house with family, servants, errant daughters and grandchildren. The Home Guard filled the fields with their silver barrage balloons. The war had been a struggle in other ways too. Philip had relations in Germany. Now they were erased from our lives. "We no longer know them," said Edith tight-lipped. Only one came home, Philip's sister Louise, left penniless by war and her husband's death in Bremen. Uncle Herman was wheeled to his grave in a stolen wheelbarrow. Wheelbarrows were hard to get hold of in war-torn Bremen.

For a child the cottage was paradise. It had been an old farm. The barns remained but three cottages had been turned into one dwelling with an extra wing added on. There was freedom to explore and no leopards to eat my dog. What terrified me most were the bats who flew into my bedroom at night. Even in the terrible winter of 1947, the garden was beautiful with its graceful cedars of Lebanon and frozen ponds. I spent hours with the gardener chatting mercilessly, not realizing that he was deaf. I loved the greenhouses, the vegetable gardens and the orchards. My daily pleasure was to climb onto a chair and reach for the musical Toby jug in the porch. I would play the refrain over and over before I ran out into the cold to search for John Peel in his red coat.

D'ye ken John Peel with his coat so gay?
D'ye ken John Peel at the break of day?
D'ye ken John Peel when he's far, far away,
With his hounds and his horn in the morning?

The hunting horn was an evocative sound in the Kent winter mornings for a child used to the noises of an African night. There were other attractions too, a natural history museum in the garage, chickens, ducks, two pigs, dogs and stables where I could go and pet the horses. The rabbits had all been turned into casseroles. And there were the exotic inhabitants, you couldn't call them pets – the falcons. This was another of the family's passions. Grandfather Philip, my father and my uncle were founding members of the British Falconers Club. Before the war they used to travel to Scotland in search of nestlings from abandoned nests. Many chicks whose lives were threatened by hunters and farmers were saved in this way.

Members of the British Falconers Club outside the Red Lion pub, Avebury

The keepers on the large estates would phone the club and report available chicks. The most famous member of this club was Captain Charles Knight, known as Unk, who wrote a book on the golden eagle. Unk had fought at Ypres and on the Somme, winning the Military Cross and gaining a reputation as Sniper Knight. His war wasn't only spent sniping. In the gaps between the skirmishes, he sheltered in barns, where he sought comfort sketching the bird life. The group flew merlins, sparrowhawks, goshawks and peregrines with romantic names like Melisande, Marmaduke, Helga, Drusilla and Javert. One particularly war-like bird was called Bellicosis. Unk went one better. His golden eagle, christened Mr Ramshaw by his five-year-old daughter, was discovered in a London zoo. He became Unk's companion for the next thirty years, replacing a wife who died young. Mr Ramshaw, like his owner, enjoyed drama. He liked to attack armchairs and both he and Unk took parts in films in the 1950s. The bird became a celebrity, especially in America, where he had an embarrassing tendency to go fly-about. As the hotels would not allow eagles in the bedrooms, Mr Ramshaw was chained up on the roof. Once, in New York, he escaped. A police alert went out to apprehend him after a call from a hysterical passer-by reporting that she had seen a real live eagle riding on the roof of a taxi. On that same visit Unk acquired Miss America, an American bald eagle. But Miss America proved too unruly and ended up in the London zoo. Mr Ramshaw too had moments of rebellion. During a lecture in an NBC studio, he took off and flew around the studio defecating generously as the studio team ran for cover. Even his usual treat of chicken heads didn't bring him to order. The war nearly got him, however. When Unk sailed to America in a Dutch boat in 1940, they were torpedoed and the call went up to abandon ship. Unk refused to abandon his bird.

"A bird?" exclaimed the Dutch captain. "You want to die for a bird?"

He pushed Unk into the lifeboat and rowed away as the ship

listed dangerously. A watery end seemed inappropriate for such a magnificent hero of the air. Unk feared the worst. Some days later he got a call.

"We've towed your boat to Scotland," said a Scottish voice. "We've found an eagle. It's still alive, but only just. You'd better come and collect him."

Unk raced to Scotland, where he found a soggy Mr Ramshaw trapped in his floating cage, inches from the ceiling in a half-sunken boat that had been towed to harbour.

"Hello, old boy," said Unk.

"Toot toot," replied Mr Ramshaw.

It was said by Unk that this was the only time the bird was pleased to see him.

Members of this select club included other figures like Jack Mavrogordato, ex attorney-general in the Sudan, who looked like an Old Testament prophet with his long black beard. We children called him Jesus Christ. When we met him later in the 1950s he had retired to a cottage in Wiltshire with his Sudanese bearer and numerous hawks. It wasn't your normal front garden in Tisbury. There were no flowering borders. The lawn sprouted posts, each occupied by a hawk whose head swivelled in our direction as we opened the gate, assessing us with yellow-ringed eyes. Among them was an eagle owl, three feet high with a wingspan of six feet. We liked Jack but we weren't sure about the birds. We left them well alone. Another member of this group was the artist George Lodge, who painted pictures of members' falcons. Grandpa Philip also painted his own versions. The Salisbury Plain and Avebury were favourite hunting grounds for rooks and rabbits and there were visits to the Isle of Sheppey and hawking holidays in Devon. Things were not the same after the Second World War. Some members never returned. Unk died in 1957, outlived by Mr Ramshaw by four months – they were together for longer than many marriages. Most of the hawks were eventually returned to the wild. Despite the long years of sitting up at night trying to train them, you could never completely tame them.

Philip was famous for solving a birding riddle. Snipe make a humming vibrato sound unlike any other bird. No one knew why. Philip, who loved a bit of theatre, demonstrated his findings at a British Ornithologists' Club dinner in 1931. He attached two outer tail feathers to a cork at a 180-degree angle to the direction of flight and whirled it dramatically around his head until Pagani's restaurant resonated to the sound of the wetlands. He proved that as the bird dived, its tail feathers made the drumming sound whereas the vibrato came from the wings. He had other ornithological discoveries to his name but none so theatrical.

Although my mother Joan was warmly welcomed into the family, she wasn't the daughter-in-law they might have expected. She was an exotic bird blown in on the wind. Her background and life experience couldn't be more different from theirs. She had grown up in a small town in Scotland impoverished by war and the Spanish flu but had escaped to South Africa as a girl. She hated the country, all that mud and mist. She was an urban girl who liked shops and shoes. She thought the county girls dowdy and the British love of animals passed her by. She could never understand field sports and had no wish to ride a horse. And she could never understand why everyone rushed to clean the house before Mrs Whitebread came to work. A cleaner was supposed to clean, not gossip over cups of tea. Edith, desperate to keep one son at home, bought a house for Joan and Clinton within walking distance. It was large, 1920s and warmer than the cottage. Philip offered Clinton a job in Harley Street. But the daily commute from Westerham was no substitute for dusty drives across the African plain and often Philip forgot to pay his salary. Clinton looked for other work. Even ordinary medical work was hard to find after the war. It was the offer of a position in Bournemouth that made up his mind. When Edith died suddenly, there was nothing to keep him in England. Clinton sold the house and rejoined the Colonial Service. He hoped for Kenya but was offered the Fiji Islands. It wasn't what Joan wanted either but it was better than Bournemouth and about as far away as you could go.

Philip's watercolour of the drumming of the snipe

THE GIRL FROM SALTCOATS

1915–1943

Joan as a FANY in Kenya

The fairies who gathered around Joan's cradle in 1915 brought unwelcome gifts of sickness and death. One, however, must have felt pity for the child in the shabby house in Canal Street in Saltcoats, for she gave her the tools to deal with her fate: cheerfulness, common sense and the ability to adapt. The house is still there, a top-heavy building on the edge of the canal. It is still unremittingly ugly. It was a terrible time to be born, in the middle of the First World War. The baby was christened Joanna McGuffie McInnes. She was three when her parents and baby sister died of Spanish flu, the same year her future father-in-law, Philip, was eradicating cholera among the troops in Egypt. Joan was passed like a parcel around the family from great-aunt to great-aunt until she forgot her own name. For some reason, Joan's grandmother Janet didn't take the child – she was sixty at the time and having borne ten children, seven of whom died, probably didn't have the energy to care for another. Or perhaps it was because she didn't approve of Joan's father, Norman McInnes, for she didn't go to the wedding. Nor did she sign her daughter's death certificate.

The Spanish flu killed mainly the young and active, like Joan's parents, and it came in 1918 as a cruel epilogue to the First World War. Scotland, where Joan grew up, was one of the worst affected areas. The virus spread quickly among a malnourished population exhausted by war. There is no doubt it travelled with the war, perhaps from the 135,000 Chinese labourers who dug the trenches. Some say that it started in a farm in Kansas and travelled with the Americans since many cases were linked to the arrival of their troops in Europe.

The high death rate (the world death toll is thought to be over fifty million) was also the result of scarce medical facilities since most doctors were serving in the war. Of the elderly doctors brought out of retirement in Scotland, many died on the job, sometimes dropping dead in the street. Houses with gates covered with flies indicated what lay inside. The flu spread everywhere – Philip encountered it in Palestine in 1918. In Ethiopia it was called 'disease of the wind' for its destructive spread. Even the baboons died, their corpses littering the plains like Buddhist mounds. Perhaps this terrible legacy was the reason that Joan never spoke of her childhood. When the elderly aunts too died off, she went to live with her grandmother at a house called Mizpah in Dynamite Road, Stevenston, on the east coast of the Firth of Clyde. At the bottom of Dynamite Road, on 100 acres of desolate sand dunes, was a factory known as 'The Dynamite', producing explosives, belonging to Nobel Enterprises. Later it became part of ICI. At the time the factory employed 3,000 men and women. Mizpah ('Watchtower' in Hebrew) had previously been occupied by one Alexander Brown, who was killed in an explosion at the factory in 1913 where eight men died and several were wounded. The explosion could be heard miles away and the smoke and dust lingered for days. There were many previous explosions at the factory, for nitroglycerine was notoriously dangerous. Later the factory produced dynamite invented by Alfred Nobel. Dynamite Road as seen in postcards of the time was a drab street lined with small semi-detached cottages dominated by industrial towers. There were some escapes, like the beach, the golf course, the hills behind the town, and occasionally over the sea to Arran.

By 1915 when Joan was born, Stevenston no longer suffered regular outbreaks of cholera. In one outbreak in 1849 so many died that special cholera pits were built to bury them. The 'Dynamite' turned Stevenston into a busy little town perched between the hills and the sea. There were cabinet makers, dress shops, milliners, vintners and a pawn shop run by Joan's grandfather John Taylor, an ex-merchant seaman. The town had a railway (closed down during the war), a canal, thirty-two coal mines and a quarry producing high quality white sandstone. There was even a Ritz ballroom and it was said that the town was so safe that young girls could walk home alone at night. However, by 1922 all that had changed with high unemployment in the three towns along the canal, and even in the 1940s many houses still lacked electricity. Since no one, including Joan, ever spoke about her father, Norman, we were never sure what he did for a living. Listed on his marriage certificate as a bricklayer, he might well have worked for Nobel, and if he had, it might explain how the flu came into the family, for munitions factories and mines were hit heavily by the virus. No one ever mentioned him. It was as if he had never existed. Life was strict, no alcohol, church on Sundays. Joan remembered long sermons and fires lit on church days when she sat upright in a stiff chair waiting for something to happen, only it didn't. There had been a sunny moment when she was given a banana. She never forgot its taste. She spoke once of a visit to the Isle of Arran just over the sea. It was as if she had crossed to the other side of the world. When she went to live at Mizpah, her grandmother Janet was already a widow. It cannot have been an easy life for either of them. Janet became ill with the stomach cancer that killed her at seventy-three, leaving thirteen-year-old Joan an orphan for the second time. She left a small legacy for the girl to see the world. She herself had gone no further afield than Belfast.

Joan left in 1928 with her aunt Georgina, who was emigrating to South Africa. An older aunt was already settled in Durban. They sailed on a Union-Castle ship crowded with families escaping Britain. Unlike the well-to-do Mansons who filled jobs in the Empire, Joan's aunts went abroad for a better life. Aunt Bessie and Uncle Tom bought land on the edge of Durban. They cleared the bush, built a house and opened a convenience store. This was unusual for Europeans since most stores were run by Indians. It was a happy family with five girls and one boy. Life continued much as it had done in Ayrshire. There was still church on Sunday but it didn't seem so dull with the sun shining outside. There was school, holidays at the coast and parties with cousins. The family flourished under the South African sun. At twenty-one Joan came into her small legacy (she pretended it was larger than it was). Remembering her grandmother's advice to travel, she left her job as a secretary and planned her trip. Paris, New York and London were top of the list.

"Respectable girls don't travel alone," insisted Uncle Tom.

Aunt Bessie urged her to keep the money for her marriage – there had already been suitors. But no, Joan was off, back on Union-Castle wearing clothes she had copied from fashion magazines and had made up by Indian tailors. She knew what suited her. She was pear-shaped with a small waist, green eyes, thick chestnut hair and an impeccable Scottish complexion which she protected all her life. She never liked her teeth which protruded charmingly and made sure her children's teeth were straight. "No man will want you with crooked teeth," she warned me. I wore braces for years.

She left Durban in 1936. The whole family came to see her off in the elegant ship with its lilac bottom and black and orange funnel, its gilded saloons and its curving staircases with thirties murals. It was a brave step. Joan was twenty-one. South Africa was her home and Aunt Bessie and Uncle Tom her family. She hoped to return. But adventures do not always end the way they are planned.

The ship sailed south, stopping off at ports along the east coast of Africa: Richards Bay, Port Elizabeth, East London, Cape Town and on around the Cape of Good Hope, last stop Madeira before berthing at Southampton. Joan started to reinvent herself. She visited London and Paris. She sailed first class to New York on the *Queen Mary* and wondered why so many men pursued her. A single woman travelling with a surplus of trunks was a glorious target for fortune hunters. But her common sense prevailed. She managed a trip to Scotland to visit two spinster aunts who lived in genteel poverty in Glasgow. It was an awkward visit. They kept their hats on and expressed shock that Joan worked as a typist. Horrified by their not-so-genteel poverty, Joan rushed back to London. She had already grown away from her roots. She never returned. Even in old age, she wanted nothing to do with her past. Now her funds were running low and there was the threat of another war. She packed her trunks with her dresses and shoes and boarded a Union-Castle ship where she found herself sharing a cabin with Betty, a tall red-headed girl who had just graduated from the Webber Douglas School of Drama. At Mombasa, Joan broke her journey and travelled on the overnight train with Betty to her family farm in the White Highlands. When the railway was started in 1885 it was fraught with problems, not least the lions picking off its Indian workers. The lions were shot and the line opened in 1901. Now the train smoked its slow, safe way from the rich coastal forests up through the plains swarming with game.

At Nairobi, Betty's step-father, Uncle Herman, met them and drove them along the road above the Rift Valley to his farm in Subukia, 'beautiful place' in the Maasai language. And it was beautiful with its grasslands and forests. A thousand acres at 6,500ft above sea level, it was a bit like the Cotswolds with more space, bigger skies and without the rules. Joan was enchanted. Here she could reinvent herself. Like Alice in Wonderland she had fallen into a magic world. Maryland was the home of Mollie and Herman Eckstein, who held open house every Sunday. Herman took the church service and Mollie, who had been a concert pianist, played the piano. Everyone stayed for lunch and some overnight, even when the beds ran out, which they often did, for the farmhouse was a cramped wooden bungalow overgrown with extensions. And not only were there people, but there were also horses and a tribe of Great Danes to fill the spaces. Had it not been for its bucolic setting and the chattering of the monkeys, the house would have been considered no better than a beach bungalow in England. Joan would never have guessed that Herman was seriously rich. Despite his German name, Herman was born in Wiltshire and had gone to Eton. He had served as a captain in the 17th Lancers but made his money on the Rand in South Africa. At one time his firm controlled half its gold mines. In 1919 he acquired his thousand acres under the Soldier Settlement Scheme after the First World War in which he had served. While at a concert in South Africa, he took a shine to the pianist and married her. Not only had Herman made his own fortune, but he had also inherited one, and yet, like many settlers, he lived simply on his acres. This was no Happy Valley set of swapped beds or keys thrown into bowls at the end of a drunken evening. Everyone knew the members of that set. One of Clinton's doctor friends found Lord Errol's body slumped in his car early one morning in 1942. Thinking Errol drunk, he moved the body and destroyed some of the evidence. But Herman was no playboy. He was involved in mining as a director of Kenya Consolidated Goldfields. This was a world that Joan slotted easily into. There were all the comforts of settler life, the Nyeri Golf Club, the Aberdare Country Club and, closer to Nairobi, the Muthaiga Club, the favourite haunt of the Happy Valley set. Here they danced all night and drank champagne and gin for breakfast. It was a bit like the Bullingdon Club – do what you like but pay for the damage. Lord Delamere, the club's first president, was rumoured to have ridden his horse into the dining room while firing his gun.

Every day brought pleasures, from the misty sunrise to the purple jacarandas, the silver eucalyptus, the bright clothes of the African women and sundowners at dusk as Joan watched the fat orange sun sink below the horizon. But this beautiful place had a sad history. These highlands had been the preserve of the nomadic Maasai. In 1897 the rains failed, causing drought and famine. This was followed by smallpox and rinderpest, leading to the deaths of two-thirds of the Maasai and most of their cattle. By 1904 the remaining members of the tribe were moved into reserves. The colonial government saw these grasslands as uninhabited and therefore available for settlement. The policy then was to use unoccupied land but it was sometimes difficult to prove ownership as some of the lands were left fallow for years. Many of the farms in the 'white highlands' were on old Maasai grazing grounds. In 1911 the remaining Maasai were evicted from their 'beautiful place' in Subukia. Molly always said that there were ghosts in her rose garden, those tall, elegant warriors returning to dance in their old haunts. Joan probably didn't give much thought to its history. Did Herman question the origins of his farm? Like the British colonial government, he saw these rich lands going to waste. Herman wasn't an unthinking man and he was a generous one. He gave much of his money away to the Oxford Group, known as Moral Re-Armament, a religious group that swallowed up donations, leaving his own family short of funds at the end of their lives.

Some of the settlers became more British than those at home. The customs of the old country continued, with old Etonian dinners, St George's Day celebrations and Caledonian dinners where every kilt in Kenya came out of mothballs. There was hunting with imported hounds and trout fishing in the highland streams, the fish imported from Britain and gleefully poached by the locals. Joan had travelled a long way to find Subukia. But even in 1940, there were hints of troubles to come. Betty's sister Joan was attacked while out riding on the farm. One night the cook ran amok with a kitchen knife but it turned out to be nothing more sinister than a witchdoctor's spell. The resentment against colonialism festered. The Second World War had reached Italian Somalia and Ethiopia. The Germans were in Tanzania (Tanganyika). Betty and Joan couldn't play golf and party forever. They signed up for the FANYs. Neither of them knew anything about first aid. But they could drive and they could type.

The FANYs (Women's First Aid Nursing Yeomanry) was the result of a dream. In 1898 in the Sudan, Edward Baker, a wounded cavalry sergeant-major fighting with Lord Kitchener, had a vision of nurses riding over the desert on horseback; an erotic dream, perhaps, but with a useful ending. In the morning, with the dream still vivid, the sergeant-major decided to turn it into reality and create a female army unit, 'a missing link', as he put it, between the front and the base. It took him nine years to found his unit of field nurses, although on motorbikes and trucks, not on horses. By 1942 the FANYs were a well-established unit with a distinguished record during the First World War. Some described them as 'posh girls driving cars'. Their six hundred members included recruits from Canada, Australia, New Zealand, Cyprus, Mauritius and Colonial Africa. Some worked in Britain, some at Bletchley, others as highly trained PAs with important positions. Some worked in the Wrens and the RAF. They packed parachutes, dragged the wounded from burning buildings and drove ambulances. Some were involved in SOE operations. Thirty-nine women were dropped into occupied France where they worked with General de Gaulle's Free French and operated heavy wireless sets, tapping the Morse code at the lightning speed of twenty-five words a minute. Violette Szabo and Noor Inayat Khan died in concentration camps. One FANY died in Belsen just as the camp was freed by the British. Several drowned when their ship was torpedoed off the coast of East Africa.

Joan and Betty were not seeking heroism. They wanted a job. They both agreed that the uniform did them no favours. What girl looked good in khaki? But they signed up and joined a committed and efficient group of women working as typists, drivers, mechanics, nurses and dispatch drivers on noisy motorbikes. There were complaints about women bombing about Nairobi on their machines. Compared to what the FANYs did elsewhere, Kenya seemed a bit of a holiday. Friendships among the women lasted for life. My brother and I benefitted from this female network when we moved to London, where we knew no one. One of Joan's FANY friends took us under her wing and introduced us to 'society'. My brother was, for a time, a 'debs' delight'. The parties and the girls brightened up his student days at St Thomas' Hospital.

When the war against Italian Somalia and Abyssinia ended in late 1941, it left the colony with the problem of 58,000 Italian prisoners of war to be fed and housed at a time when there were severe food shortages and a lack of officers to run the camps. Some prisoners were employed on the farms, but they were more expensive to hire than African labour. There was a fixed minimum wage for prisoners of war but not for African workers. The FANYs stepped in. Some, like the two girls sent to manage a camp full of women and children high up on the Mau summit, were very young. They found wooden shacks with gaps in the walls and doors that didn't fit – this was in freezing temperatures. Shortages of food made the girls' lives even more difficult. When soldiers from the King's African Rifles were sent to help, there were racist complaints from the prisoners. The most famous Italian prisoner of war was Amadeo, Duke of Aosta, a cousin of the King of Italy who died of malaria and tuberculosis. Amadeo had been educated in Britain, spoke pukka English and enjoyed fox hunting and polo. He is buried in a tiny Italian church in Nyeri not far from Subukia.

Joan and Betty were stationed at barracks in Gilgil, a dusty town on the edge of the eastern wall of the Rift Valley, four kilometres from the soda lake of Elementaita. 'Ol muteita', from which the lake was named, meant 'dusty place' in Maasai. These, too, had been Maasai lands. Gilgil looked like some western cowboy town put up in a hurry and weathered by the relentless wind. But it did boast a country club set in beautiful gardens, which was a magnet for the European men and women stationed there. Joan divided her time between typing and driving officers up and down the Rift Valley roads. There were parties with dancing and Scottish reels (which much impressed the Maasai). And there were weddings as FANYs fell one by one on the altar of marriage. Joan was in no hurry. Life was too much fun. Clinton wasn't really her sort of man. But the war was coming to an end and there were decisions to be made. Besides, her money was running out. Did she see a good prospect,

FANY wedding. Betty as bride; Joan on her left

a doctor whose father was a Knight of the Realm, a step up for the girl from Saltcoats? Perhaps they simply liked each other – opposites who found each other attractive. Clinton was the product of a male public school where the only women were menopausal matrons. He liked shooting and mud and dirt and wild open places where there were no shops. He talked well but was never at ease with women. He felt most at home among men. They married without knowing very much about each other but the war was full of such marriages. Perhaps Clinton admired Joan for her guts and her adventurous spirit. Men like Clinton didn't look for soul mates, nor did they seek intellectual companions. In Clinton's case it was altogether more practical. He wanted a wife who would give him children and take care of the domestic issues, leaving him free to concentrate on his research. Later in life Clinton was heard to say he chose Joan because 'she looked fertile'. They married in January 1943 at St Andrew's

Anglican Church in Nyeri, a small piece of England planted in the rough red soil of Africa. None of Joan's family were present. Uncle Herman gave her away and hosted the reception at Maryland, which they shared with the Maasai ghosts in the rose garden. Afterwards they left for a honeymoon at Thomson's Falls, staying in what Joan described as a shack but was probably a cabin belonging to the local fishing lodge. Clinton didn't go in for hotels. As Joan told it, Clinton sat on the long drop and shot the dinner. They ate eland steaks by lamplight while Clinton sorted out the next day's fishing. It was not what she expected. She had dressed for dinner in her new frock, copied from *Vogue* magazine, with stockings and high heels, which Clinton failed to notice. But she had learnt that life in Kenya was never what you expected. Besides, it was early days, the country was beautiful and there was plenty of time to sit around and count the stars in the deep black night. She saw her life in Kenya as never-ending. It was where she had signed up to stay. She didn't expect to move to cold post-war England within four years. Nor did she choose our next posting five years later, the hot and humid Pacific island of Fiji, where Clinton was sent by the Colonial Service in 1948. It was at the other end of the world, and besides, she hated the heat almost as much as she hated the cold.

As for the FANYs, they continued working into the 1980s, on call to the City of London Police Major Incident Unit. They were present at the Moorgate Tube disaster and the IRA bomb attack at Bishopsgate in 1993. During Covid they supported the senior matron team at the Royal London Hospital's Adult Critical Care Unit. A memorial to those who died in East Africa is on the north wall of St Paul's Church Wilton Place, London.

RETURN TO THE PACIFIC

1948–1953

Medical students, Suva, 1950 – Philip third left. Clinton second right

When we arrived in Suva, thirty-eight years after Philip's visit, the eating of human flesh was forbidden but not forgotten. My father took me on a visit to a remote village in the mountains – the roads were much improved since Philip's time. A man gnarled and shrivelled with age crouched beside me. He had, he said, "eaten the flesh of missionary". He grinned when he saw the horror on my face. "I got the toe". Perhaps he had eaten the toe of Thomas Baker, an ardent converter of men who was devoured in 1867. Only his bones were left. Even his shoes were nibbled. I didn't know about Thomas Baker but I remember my fear turning to the thrill of forbidden knowledge. This corpse-like ancient wasn't what I expected cannibals to look like. Cannibalism wasn't a way of adding protein to the diet. You ate your enemy because you hated him. Or in the case of Thomas Baker, because he had pulled a comb from the chief's hair, unaware that the head was sacred. Although missionaries in the 19th century said that 'Fiji was a paradise wasted on savage cannibals', Philip discovered that it wasn't paradise. Thor Heyerdahl had expected to find his Garden of Eden on the island of Fatu Hiva. Sadly he was disabused, shocked by disease and hostile inhabitants. However, for us children post-war Fiji was a paradise of deserted beaches, swimming parties, boat trips to islands, Sunday lunch in the Grand Pacific Hotel eating iced melon and papaya, and gardens with enormous fig trees whose creeping roots made dens for small people. I had a swing on the largest ficus tree, where I used to sit and recite Robert Louis Stevenson's poems. He had lived and died in Samoa, not far away in Pacific terms, surrounded by the same trees. I felt very close to him.

Our house would not have looked out of place in the Home Counties, a functional 1930s two-storey building with Crittall windows surrounded by a garden of mango, coconut and ficus trees. There was just too much rain in Suva. It was measured in feet. "Bath day," our gardener used to say as he stood under it in his white dhoti. But it brought a bright palette of colours and leaves that weren't all green. It also brought fertile soil. The islands hadn't suffered famines; you could see the evidence in the strong build of its people. Body mass was valued in the Pacific. The fatter you were the nobler your lineage. Queen Salote of Tonga, the grandest of them all, had to have special furniture made for her at school in New Zealand. We didn't need orange boxes like Philip. Our house came furnished with Public Works Department furniture, the sort you might find in house clearances. My mother, Joan, terrorized the employees of the PWD warehouses with demands for something better. She became adept at covering boxes with fabric to turn them into dressing tables and upholstered sofas and chairs with denim before it became fashionable, using her faithful Singer sewing machine. We owned very little apart from the machine and a few bits of linen and crockery. We were nomads accumulating memories as the house accumulated cockroaches – armies of them, leftovers from 320 million years with no desire to become extinct.

Fijian society was communal, possessions shared. If a Fijian admired your possessions it was hoped that you might hand them over. The Indians were ambitious and hard-working. They had a tough history. Most of them were untouchables who wanted a better life even if indentured labour was little better than slavery; 60,000 came over between 1875 and 1916, many dying on the voyage over from cholera and smallpox. They came on five-year contracts, enduring unpaid wages, beatings, crowded accommodation and disease. At the end of their term they could return, but if they stayed ten years their passage home was paid. Many chose to remain. Some became farmers leasing tribal land. Many turned into traders and shopkeepers. Some worked as clerks and administrators for the colonial government. Later generations became doctors, dentists, business leaders and politicians. The Fijians didn't like being servants. Under their tribal system, they didn't have to work at all. They might come and work for a month or so and then go back to their village. They might reappear, send a replacement or just vanish. My brother and I liked our Fijian maids. We loved their generous curves, their smiling faces and their halos of black hair, which required a special comb to keep it in order. They were exciting. They took us on adventures. They taught us Fijian songs. One who lasted longer than the others had lovers who would call at night when our parents were out. When I couldn't sleep, I would wander down to her room and invariably find someone there. They were always kind to me. When my mother found out, the maid was banished. She left proudly carrying her suitcase with not a care in the world. Why work if you didn't have to? There was also a lover who worked on a boat in the harbour. Out would come the lemonade in a murky-looking bottle. When I woke after a suspiciously deep sleep some hours later, it was time to go home. "Don't tell your mother," whispered the maid. Another secret to add to the list.

The Indians, however, made wonderful servants. One day Joan announced that she must have a cook. It was too much, all that cooking and entertaining. She hated cooking. Clinton returned home for lunch most days and finished work at tea time. And there were the dinner parties. Colonial life was rigorously social. Despite my father's protestations, Mari appeared in answer to an advertisement. Mari was a tall, gaunt Indian who looked older than he was. He was very dark and very thin with a friendly face and warm brown eyes. When he smiled his wide toothy grin, we knew immediately that he would fit in. He could cook anything except curries. Mari had a small farm rented from Fijians. He worked eleven months for us and returned for the odd weekend and one month a year to help his wife and children with the farm. By Fijian standards, he was expensive but he was a prodigious worker. His soufflés, specially the chocolate, were five star. He made the cakes for our birthdays. There were ship cakes, ladies with crinolines, trains and cars. Mari organized all our entertainment. For our parties he would set up a long table under the broadest fig tree. A blow-up army raft from the war was turned into a paddling pool. A friend of his arrived with a wretched-looking horse, which took us for rides around the garden. Many people tried to poach Mari. Even Government House offered him a job but he wouldn't leave my mother. He had his own quarters and the use of the kitchen, where he cooked his chapatis and vegetables. Like the gardener Baba, he was Hindu. Baba, so old he looked immortal, shared his chapatis with me. He insisted on respect for his age and wisdom. Baba meant 'wise man', and he was wise. He sat on the ground like a guru, knees not quite in the lotus position, slowly eating his chapatis, tearing off bits for me. Both Mari and Baba were descendants of indentured labourers.

Our food was all local, bought fresh daily from the market in town. Perishables were kept in an ice box refilled regularly with ice. We didn't have a fridge. What we did have was space, lots of it. Our beaches were empty. There were no tourists. Every weekend there would be an outing to a local island to picnic and swim. An island not known for its beaches was Levuka, which Philip also visited. Now it is home to Chinese tuna canning factories. But its Somerset Maugham charm remains in its sleepy hotels and lethargic expats and it is now a UNESCO World Heritage Site. Our favourite local treat in Suva was a visit to Colo-i-Suva, a mini rain forest on the edge of town, which had hot springs and cold pools. You could jump from one to the other and slide down the waterfalls. Visitors to Suva included the Royal Navy, who gave wonderful children's parties on board, with cakes and lemonade, and let us children rampage all over the ships. There was one department store in Suva, Morris Hedstrom, who sold everything from Afghan rugs to English china. Joan bought her Chinese furniture there and after lusting after a family of celadon ducks, gave in and bought the lot. A newspaper, *The Fiji Times*, published the New Year's Honours list from London. These were always carefully scrutinized although out of date by the time we got them. The comments were often bitchy. There was one newly created lady who was much disliked by the other memsahibs. The response was predictably cutting.

"What could the King do that even the Lord God Almighty couldn't do…" (laughter all round) "make a lady out of Mrs Parker-Allen."

Every afternoon at four Joan changed into a tea frock to greet Clinton when he came home. Joan's worst fear was to let standards slip, especially in the colonies, where, if you were white, you were supposed to set a good example. And besides, as everyone knew,

Wedding at the Grand Pacific Hotel – author as bridesmaid

single women in the colonies were skillful poachers of husbands. A treat for us children was to stay up late for events like wedding receptions at the Grand Pacific Hotel. Everyone dressed up, the women in long dresses, the men in dinner jackets. Sometimes tippets of fur appeared to keep out the mild night air. We children would sit on the verandas with our lemonade, listening to the band and the rustling of the palms, knowing that it was way past our bedtime. On nights like that when the sea was calm, lapping gently on the beach below us, it was hard to believe that this very same sea could turn brutal and batter the coast in a tsunami. Among forbidden treats was tamarind paste. It looked like pressed dates, tasted both sweet and salty, and came wrapped in old newspaper. It was considered unhygienic. Newspapers were commonly used as lavatory paper and who knew where the paper had been stored. I spent my Brownie money and ate my purchase until I was found out.

School was relaxed with plenty of time to dream. The classes were small and there was no pressure of exams. I wore starched linen shirt dresses in pale blue or pink with matching ribbons on my plaits, white socks and Mary Jane shoes. My mother would drive me in a bouncy old Ford down the winding road to the sea, past avenues of fiery flame trees, past the Grand Pacific Hotel, past the municipal pool where I swam most afternoons. We had many breaks in lessons, not only for holidays but also whenever a hurricane approached and the black warning flag was raised. Then we went home, the shutters came down and we sat it out. Any pupil could attend our school if they had a British grandparent. Those who didn't qualify, like the Indians, went to the Catholic convent. How I envied the Indian girls in their frilly dresses, all sparkle and colour with pretty clips in their hair. When I begged for a party dress, I expected the same. What arrived from the Indian tailor was restrained pink organza with neat tucks and not a sparkle to be seen.

There was a pecking order in the Colonial Service and we all knew it. Doctors were at the top, policemen at the bottom and other races even further down. The Fijians, however, had no feelings of inferiority. No one looked down on them because of their race. Their tribal society was just as class ridden. There were the nobles and the others. Society was run by hereditary chiefs who distributed the clan land as they thought fit. No one owned the land and in theory no one went without. Colonial society was equally tribal. The same people went to the same parties. They joined the same clubs. They performed in the same plays. They sang in choirs together. Their children went to the same schools. They ate Sunday lunch in the Grand Pacific Hotel. In Holy Trinity Cathedral, where we went to church, we found a more diverse group but they were not invited to our parties. And yet there was comfort in knowing everyone, of being a member of the tribe even if there was snobbery in the ranks. As a child, I do remember feeling lucky for being British and sorry for those who weren't. I belonged to the pink world I could see on the map at school, the world of my stamps. You could travel anywhere safely in that world – like a Roman in the Empire. Despite the different cultures and languages, you would fit in. We were never taught anything about the cultures of the other people who lived in our Empire. Most of us colonials in Fiji were British, this included Australians and New Zealanders, but some were European. Clinton had a friend, a Polish doctor, who had joined the service and asked to be sent as far away from Europe as possible. During the Second World War, when the Russians invaded Warsaw, he saw his wife killed and his fourteen-year-old daughter gang-raped by soldiers in the Red Army. He never spoke of it. His life in Fiji included a new family.

Like all Gardens of Eden, this one had its serpents. Many types of sea snakes live in the Pacific Ocean, all of them venomous. The most deadly was the banded sea krait, which lived on the coral reefs but spent some time on land. Sometimes when we went snorkelling we saw snakes but we kept a wide berth. The stone fish was just as lethal. By the time you had stepped on it, it was too late. Other nasty creatures lived in the tidal pools in the reef. So we didn't put our hands into the pools. Sharks tended to stay further out. An unpleasant immigrant was the warty cane toad brought from Asia to control insects in the sugar cane fields. By the time we reached Fiji it had bred out of control. Apart from its size, that of a large dinner plate, its skin was toxic and hallucinogenic. The very brave or the most addicted liked to run their tongues along their surface to get high. Sometimes there were plagues of toads. At night you could find yourself slipping and sliding on their churning bodies.

We were spoiled for choice with our beaches, where we would swim or sit on the sand with our buckets and spades and gaze at the white fringe of waves breaking on the reef that protected us from the ocean. Sometimes we had the use of a wooden shack with no electricity or running water and a long drop lavatory, like the shack Philip and Edith had lived in. It had shutters, mosquito netting (there were plenty of mosquitoes in Fiji) and a verandah, which fronted onto the tracks of the sugar cane railway. We children loved it – it was real *Robinson Crusoe*, only we had no wish to be rescued. On the other side of the tracks was the beach, our beach, for there was no one else on it. Joan would sit in the shade of the palm trees under an enormous sun hat. She kept well clear of the sea and the sun. The sugar cane train would pass by several times a day. The Indian engine driver always tooted hello. At night we had hurricane lamps, which attracted all the flying insects. We had the use of a boat and motored out to islands or up the creeks of mangrove swamps. Their spreading roots, home to turtles, lizards, crabs, small fish, extended deep beneath the surface and protected the coast from storm surges. As we cruised among the swamps, there would be a chorus of 'yucks' as we covered our noses with our hands to keep out the sulphuric smell of rotten eggs. Now they are threatened habitats and the coast of Fiji is crumbling where they have died, exposing the land to the whims of the ocean.

Into this comfortable world came a returning intruder, as difficult as the warty toad but not addictive or slimy. Grandfather Philip, buoyed up by the success of a lecture trip in America, arrived on another research trip. Much had changed since his visit some forty years earlier. The housing was better and the sanitary arrangements worked and he didn't have to endure five rolling days of ocean to reach us. He arrived by plane on a landing strip built on coral rock in the middle of a lagoon. As soon as he stepped from the plane a blast of air struck him, he had forgotten the shock of the humidity, but he wiped his face and concentrated on the Asiatic golden plovers flying overhead. Suva had grown, there were new hospitals and the medical students looked respectable. In Tamavua a new house and swimming pool occupied the site of his shack. Land in Suva was too expensive now for shacks. His nine acres had been tamed. All he could recognize from the old days was the lone tree that had survived the hurricane. The noisy mynah birds had spread, filling the air with their irritating chatter. Philip wanted to retrace his visit to ailing Mrs Prideaux in Sigatoka, so he and my father set off on a parasite and birding trip. Now they travelled by car. There were more people and the villages were welcoming. On return to Suva, he gave a lecture in the Grand Pacific Hotel on 'The Romance and Achievement of Tropical Medicine'. Flushed by its success, he took over Clinton's ward rounds and corrected his notes. The two men would leave together every morning, dressed in starched white shorts and a bush jacket held in at their expanding waists by a matching belt. Their long white socks and heavy shoes were quite unsuitable for the heat. They looked like Tweedledum and Tweedledee (Clinton had grown stout with the years and the beer). This 'uniform' had to be washed, starched and ironed daily. Philip became even more domineering, fawning over his new protégé, an American missionary doctor, and giving him large sums of money. We had taken an instant dislike to his children with whom we shared the school run. Joan gave him his marching orders. He packed his bags and moved into a room in the Memorial Hospital. It was more convenient, right next to the lab where he worked most nights and where he could see patients like Essau, gardener to Sir Lala Ratuna, an important Fijian chief. Sir Lala volunteered Essau as a guinea pig for research. I travelled with Philip to uninhabited Mosquito Island. In the boat were cages to trap the island's mosquitoes to see if they carried the same filarial parasites. Everyone but the captain and I went ashore clothed like bee keepers with muslin over their faces. They returned some hours later carrying cages black with mosquitoes. Now Mosquito Island is a celebrity destination that can be hired for special events. We saw little of Philip after that. He attended a Pacific conference in Suva with delegates coming from Polynesia, the French Islands, the New Hebrides and New Caledonia. A popular attendee was Prince Tungi of Tonga, Queen Salote's son. He had been educated at Sydney University, stood at 6ft 3" and was built to match. The conference was crowded. The chairs in the hall could barely support, as Philip said, "the mountains of flesh from Samoa and Tonga." Some things hadn't changed.

When Philip left on a flying boat to Sydney, everyone breathed a sigh of relief. Clinton, who hated any kind of drama, carried on with his work. Our pleasant life resumed. One hiccup was the move to a very different house, a flimsy wooden bungalow on stilts, which quivered when the wind blew. The wind blew often, for the house sat on a high ridge overlooking Walu Bay and the mountains beyond. We had to agree that the view was glorious and Clinton could walk to work up the long drive to the Colonial Memorial Hospital. Grandfather Philip had painted a watercolour of this very same view in 1910. It was close to his shack in Tamavua. The house was not up to scratch for a senior colonial official (expectations had risen since 1910) but Joan had given up harassing the public works officials. She was ill. And there was another problem. A stray cat had taken refuge underneath the house and given rise to a plague of fleas. Joan lay in bed, fading in front of us. Doctors came and went. When she began passing blood in her stools even Clinton became concerned. Was it a parasite? But which one? Joan had married into a famous tropical medical dynasty and even they couldn't discover what was wrong. Everyone knew that doctors' families were the last to be treated. It came to a head when an ambulance sped down our drive and carted her off to hospital, leaving my brother and me with Ruby, our Polish friend's wife, who came to look after us. Ruby, a devout Catholic, led us in prayers for Joan. What turned up the next day was not what we expected. A black limousine came purring down the long drive. A woman got out and immediately began scratching at her legs. Ruby peered through the mosquito netting. "Good God! It's the governor's wife!" We watched in horror as Lady Garvey stood outside in her neat suit and jacket, trying not to scratch, wondering whether to stay or to leave. She braved the fleas and we were whisked off to Government House like Cinderella in her carriage, only ours was a limo with a Union Jack flapping in the breeze and there were no horses.

Sir Ronald Garvey had just been appointed as the new governor of Fiji. A parson's son from Lincolnshire, Sir Ronald had not attended one of the major public schools, having won a choral scholarship to Trent College in Long Eaton, Derbyshire. Nor was he sporty or clubbable. But he had gone to Cambridge, where he studied history and anthropology. He had wanted to join the Indian Civil Service but hadn't been able to take time off to prepare for its tough exams. Instead he applied for a post in the Colonial Service, somewhat easier to get into, although in 1926, 400 applicants competed for twenty-seven posts. Sir Ronald's first post was the Solomon Islands, from where he moved to Suva as assistant secretary to the Western Pacific High Commission. He served in the Gilbert and Ellis Islands and Tonga and spent time in the New Hebrides. In 1939 he was sent to Tonga to persuade Queen Salote to support Britain in declaring war on Nazi Germany. This earned him an OBE. Fiji avoided a Japanese invasion in the Second World War because of the presence of a US

Navy base. After Pearl Harbour, Japanese sea planes had flown over the islands in a show of power but that was as far as they got. Fijian soldiers serving under New Zealand command in the American Solomon Islands campaign won many medals. Sir Ronald returned to Suva as governor in 1952, after an unhappy spell in Africa. A short man with round spectacles and a bow tie, he could have passed for an academic until he put on his formal dress with its gold braid and epaulettes, sashes and medals topped by an extravagantly plumed topee, when he turned into an imperial hero.

Government House, a white villa visible from the sea road, was the Buckingham Palace of Fiji, if somewhat smaller, the reigning monarch's home on the island. It was grander than the wooden long house it had replaced and was built to withstand any hurricane. It had wide verandas and a grand carriage porch with steps that led up to the main entrance. Fijian police marched up and down outside in their *sulu*s – white skirts with serrated hems, worn with blue short-sleeved shirts, a red and blue belt, and always with sandals (no socks). The rituals were faithfully observed. We children never missed the 'Last Post' played by a trumpeter at dusk as the Union Jack was lowered from the flagpole. We stood to attention, our hands at our sides, stiff with pride knowing we belonged to the parts of the world that mattered and that this very same ceremony was being played out in many other countries in our pink-hued world. There were four of us children: my brother and me and the governor's two daughters. On the nights when there were receptions we were allowed to sit on the stairs and watch the guests arrive. Sir Ronald and Lady Garvey would stand in the hall at the bottom of the stairs and receive the guests, who wore full evening dress. They were a diverse lot, Indian businessmen, colonial officers and Fijian chiefs like Ratu Sir Lala Ratuna, Speaker of the Legislative Council. Sir Lala had fought in the French Foreign Legion in the First World War, winning the Croix de Guerre. He had studied history at Oxford and later qualified as a lawyer. It was an evolution from the chiefs Philip had met in 1911. My mother admired him hugely. "Sir Lala Ratuna is a true gentleman," she would say, as if she knew him well. There were other less formal attractions to life at Government House, such as a swimming pool and an enormous tree house built by prisoners. But best of all was the daily ride to and from school in the chauffeur-driven limo, which gave me lasting ideas above my station.

The doctors who clustered around Joan's bed announced their verdict. Hookworm. This is caused by roundworms that live in the small intestine. They are passed on when the faeces of an infected person are left on ground where people might walk, or in fertilizer made from 'night soil'. They can also be ingested (one reason for not eating salads). The worm was brought to Fiji by the Indian labourers. It was thought Joan had probably picked up the infection on the beach. She recovered slowly. Her illness seemed exacerbated by the heat. She never got used to the Fijian climate. Then in 1953, the year after King George VI's death, our Pacific interlude came to an end. We had been in Suva for five years. Now we were being sent back to Kenya. Our parents were both happy to return to Africa. The move was a promotion for Clinton. I sat again with Baba in the garden for the last time, looking at the purple mountains beyond the bay that Philip had painted.

"Life, it goes round in circles… you cannot turn back."

Baba stared at me with rheumy eyes. Mari came to see us off on the ship, which would take us to Sydney from where we would take a larger liner to South Africa. Joan had found him another position. The quay throbbed with friends, relations and the curious. The band played noisily. Strings of coloured streamers hung from the railings like Christmas decorations. We climbed the gangway. People began to sing the Fijian song of farewell. I had learnt the words in Fijian. It went with the hula skirt I had for my eighth birthday, made of woven grasses, with a matching brassiere and seed rattles for my ankles. I had learnt to do the motions and made a crown and bracelets of sweet-smelling frangipane until I became Isa Lei herself:

Isa, Isa you are my only treasure
Must you leave me, so lonely and forsaken?
As the roses will miss the sun at dawn,
Every moment my heart for you is yearning.
Isa Lei, the purple shadow falling,
Sad the morrow will dawn upon my sorrow,
Oh forget not, when you're far away
Precious moments at Suva.

The horn blew. The ropes were untied. As the ship detached itself from the quay, churning the water with its propellors, the streamers snapped. I looked for Mari, my friend, my good companion, but I couldn't see him in the crowd. The tears streamed down my face. I never saw him again.

Travel in the 1950s was usually by ship, although expensive flights between London and Sydney started in 1947, with many stops on the way. Long-range planes didn't come in until 1957. Flying boats connected Fiji to Australia from the 1940s. We took one on a 'home' leave to Britain (colonial officers were given paid leave every three years). Before leaving, there was the terrifying ordeal of customs. The standard question was not "Are you carrying drugs?" but "Do you have a tabua in your luggage?" The officials had X-ray eyes. What if they found a tabua? What had Clinton done with his? Tabua, polished and shaped sperm whales' teeth, were very valuable. It was forbidden to take them out of the country. They were given as engagement, wedding or birth presents and were placed in tombs to accompany mens' spirits on the journey to the after-world.

Flying boats left from Laucala Bay west of Suva. Passengers were squashed into boats with the mail sacks and rowed out to the plane.

Sunderland flying boat
Alamy stock photo

I think ours was a Sunderland, but I don't remember. I do remember a fat-bellied plane with four propellers and a small float on each wing, waiting for us on the water. Double-decked with portholes and hatches and smelling of oil, she looked too heavy to rise from the water, and when she did, the plane seemed to sink under its own weight as the sea flooded over the portholes. There was room to walk around, with two decks connected by a spiral staircase up which we children used to scramble to the restaurant, bar and smoking room. There were bunk beds too and you could play mini-golf or quoits on the carpet and eat meals on a folding table with linen and silver service. As these planes flew at 5,000ft, we passengers had a wonderful view of the ocean and islands through the large windows. This was luxury travel. In the early days passengers could get out at stops and go fishing. In 1951, New Zealand launched the Coral Route from Auckland to Tahiti. At that time it was the only way to reach Tahiti by air. The flying boat left every Thursday from Fiji for Samoa, the Cook Islands and Papeete. In Samoa, passengers were taken in taxis to visit the coastal villages and Vailima, the home of Robert Louis Stevenson, before having dinner in a hotel. At 2am they were driven back to the plane for an early take-off for the Cook Islands, where they landed for breakfast and a swim before leaving for Papeete. Our flight was not quite as luxurious. When we touched down in Rose Bay Sydney, no one was interested in tabuas. My brother and I were made to stand up for inspection. Australia then had a strict whites only policy. We were born in Africa and had travelled from the South Pacific. "We are only in transit," commented Joan. The official was not amused.

Many shipping lines served the Empire. We travelled on them all. We had gone to Fiji in 1948 on a New Zealand Line ship crowded with families emigrating to Australia and New Zealand after the war. There was a distinct sniff of mothballs as the summer frocks came out of storage. On our way back to Kenya in 1953 we travelled in luxury on the *Dominion Monarch*. First class only, she carried 525 passengers as well as the mail. The sailors were Indian, the officers British. Most of the passengers were British but wealthy Indians used the ships too, sometimes even a prince or a maharajah. The *Dominion Monarch* was the most comfortable liner of its time, fitted out like a hotel in the Home Counties, with polished mahogany panelling, chintz furnishings and sporting prints on the walls. There was a smoking room with a fireplace and mullioned windows. Activities were designed to keep us from boredom – the journey to Cape Town took three weeks. Travelling by ship was a paid holiday, an escape from time and place. But it was no escape from the cultural and sporting pleasures of the colonials. There was dancing every night after dinner. There was deck tennis, quoits, swimming, deck games, bridge competitions, plays, parties, concerts and a fancy dress ball. Clinton dressed up as Henry VIII – in doublet and hose, with a black velvet hat – and walked around with a gilt picture frame in front of his face. It won him first prize. As the ship crossed the equator, we had a Crossing the Line ceremony. One of the largest sailors dressed up as Neptune with a hairy wig and a trident and threw us children into the swimming pool to squeals of delight. For those who spent the journey huddled in deckchairs, their only disturbance was beef tea or ices at eleven. Sometimes shoals of silver flying fish landed on the deck. Once an exhausted albatross hitched a lift and was tenderly cared for by the sailors. In port there was constant entertainment with the loading and unloading of cargoes and the comings and goings of the pilot boats.

Like the other passengers, my parents dressed for dinner. The stewards would run saltwater baths every evening. The bathrooms were not en suite. My mother wore a long dress. My father squeezed himself into his dinner jacket. It was considered an honour to sit at the captain's table. You had to be invited. People jostled to get a seat at the top table and it wasn't for the food or the conversation. The menu could have been served in any Surrey hotel.

Asparagus Mayonnaise
Fried Scampi with Tartar Sauce
Roast chicken with savoury stuffing and broad beans
Bakewell Tart and Sauce Confiture
Biscuits and Cheese
Coffee

Mulligatawny was a favourite. A legacy of India, it is usually delicious but the ship's soups came in tins and were modified for Anglo-Saxon tastes. We children had our own dining room. Its walls were covered with hand-painted murals of the ship's cat, who also featured on our menus with a different storyline each day. We had nursery fare: soup, fish, mince or roast rib of beef, fries and Brussel sprouts or peas (tinned), pies, eggs to order, fruit salad (usually tinned) with evaporated milk, ices and wafers. There was a well kitted out nursery with a Norland nurse and a deck with swings. There were books and toys. Some of the children travelled with their pets, which were kept on the pet deck where we visited them. Our journeys were broken up by mini-breaks in exotic places, too brief for some countries but too long in others. We saw snake charmers in Bombay (Mumbai) and a Parsee burial ground where the corpses were left out for the vultures. We explored as much of Sri Lanka (Ceylon) as we could in one day. On one journey via the Panama Canal, we called in at the Pitcairn Islands. There are several islands, all uninhabited except for Pitcairn, which was the island of last resort for the sailors on the *Bounty*. We anchored offshore. Long boats from Bounty Bay came out to meet us. The crew flung a rope ladder over the side. Parcels were handed up and down. Once we had the mail, we steamed away until the lonely rock became as invisible as it had been to the British Navy in 1789.

We usually had a day to linger at the ports before being enticed back to the ship by the warning sound of its sirens. Sometimes passengers turned up just in time to see us steaming away. Only once did I meet real hate. In the Suez Canal, an Egyptian labourer climbed up the mooring ropes and spat at me. I was probably eight years old. It was a shock to discover that we British were not universally liked. Mind you, we weren't keen on the Egyptians. They pestered us in port and were very adept at selling their wares and then stealing them back when we weren't looking.

On the journey to Kenya we changed ships at Cape Town to travel north up the East African coast on the *Braemar Castle*, with her distinctive lilac hull and fat black and red funnel. She too carried the mail which necessitated stops up the coast. Union-Castle mail ships (known as Union Cattle) left for Africa from Southampton every Thursday on the dot of 4pm, as regular as Swiss trains, while their twin in Cape Town left at the same time locally for the return journey. It was surprising how much history there was in each little port. Mossel Bay – Dutch for Bay of Mussels – only visited because of the mail drop, was where the first Europeans, the Portuguese, landed in 1488. We didn't go ashore. The mail and passengers were sent down in baskets to the waiting boats. East London was known more for its glorious golden beaches than for being the site of a concentration camp for Africaans woman and children during the Boer War. In Port Elizabeth we gawped at a display of elephant foetuses in the museum in all stages of gestation and wondered how many elephants had died. From Durban, where we had relatives, we went to Zanzibar. Even far out at sea we could smell the cloves. Our friend Peter, we knew him as P, the district commissioner, came out to greet us in his official launch with the Union Jack flapping in the breeze. Zanzibar had a torrid history as the centre of the East Africa slave trade. It had been part of the Sultanate of Oman and a major trading port for Arabia and India. (Slavery continued into the 20th century.) This was the same coast that great-great-grandfather James Ptolemy had patrolled in pursuit of slave ships. Somehow this tragic history seemed overlooked, perhaps because it was so old a trade yet concealed by the picturesque town with its elegant, if faded, mansions with their carved wooden doors studded with bronze. P lived in one of these graceful Arab houses, built to keep out the heat with thick walls and high ceilings. Whirring fans circulated the lazy air. Latticed shutters filtered the sun, sending shafts of light onto the glazed floor tiles. Despite its air of lethargy, Zanzibar was busy with metal workers, leather workers, porters carrying food to market and veiled women who glided past us. We wanted to stay and explore but the launch took us back before sunset. Our final stop was Mombasa, a city of mosques and muezzins smelling of spices and chargrilled corn on the cob. Towering above the harbour was the huge Portuguese Fort Jesus built in the 15th century. Five hundred years of history clung to its stones. We didn't have time to linger. We stayed only long enough to take the overnight train to Nairobi, the same train Joan had taken in 1940. Now the journey took nine hours in a smart silver train.

AFRICA AGAIN

1953–1959

Clinton with tribal elders

For Joan and Clinton, this was a return to the place of their youthful memories. But the Kenya that we returned to in 1953 was very different from the Kenya they had known. A state of emergency had been declared the previous year with the Mau Mau revolt. British troops had been sent out to restore order. There had been a brutal attack on an English family. Friends advised us not to travel there. Clinton didn't seem concerned. We would be living in Nairobi, not out in the sticks. More Africans had been murdered than Europeans. A massacre on a Kikuyu village had shocked the colony. On a moonlit night in March 1953, 400 Mau Mau crept out of the forest and surrounded the village of Lari, setting huts on fire and slaughtering cattle; 150 died, including women and children whose bodies were found in the smouldering remains the next morning. It shocked even Mau Mau supporters. Not every Kikuyu supported the guerillas, although many were forced to take the oath. Lari had been chosen because it was a loyalist village whose men had refused the oath and joined the Home Guard. The Mau Mau revolt, which had been simmering since those early days at Subukia, was about political rights and the loss of land. The Kikuyu lost most of their land, as did the Maasai. The revolt was also a reaction to the broken promises made to African veterans of both world wars. As one veteran put it,

> *"We Africans were told over and over again that we were*
> *fighting for our country and democracy and that when the*
> *war was over we would be rewarded for the sacrifice we were*

*making... The life I returned to was exactly the same as the
one I left four years earlier: no land, no job, no representation,
no dignity."*

In the 1900s the highlands had attracted settlers. Lord
Delamere, who virtually founded the colony of Kenya, saw this
empty landscape with its rich soil and good climate going to waste.
To Delamere's western mind this seemed a poor use of resources.
Delamere is an example of the white settler of his time with all the
good intentions and contradictions and hunger for cheap land. He
first visited Africa to hunt lion in Somalia, where he was severely
mauled, but saved by his Somali gun bearer. This left him with
a limp for the rest of his life. On a second visit, he walked from
the deserts of Southern Somalia into the highlands of Kenya and
saw in this fertile country an opportunity to develop the land for
grain and cattle. Despite having inherited a large estate in Cheshire,
which had been owned by the family since 1615, he saw his future
in Kenya. In 1903 he applied to the British government for a land
grant but was refused, as was his second application. At that time
the British government wanted to avoid conflict with the Maasai
whose lands these were. His third attempt resulted in a long lease
on 100,000 acres, later doubled to 200,000. Here he pioneered the
breeding of animals and developed the East African dairy industry.
But the animals succumbed to disease, as did his fields of wheat. Not
until 1914 did he begin to see some return on his investments. But it
was too late to save his estate at home. Delamere fought fiercely for
British supremacy in the colony and was one of the major recruiters
of settlers from England. He didn't see eye-to-eye with the British
government since his views were against their pro-African policy
that, in the 1923 Devonshire White Paper, declared that in Kenya,
the concerns of Africans were paramount even when they conflicted
with the needs of white settlers. The colonial government tried hard
to find solutions but the defiant settlers proved difficult to control.

Now Delamere's family is reviled by the tribe he so admired, as one who stole their land. His legacy in agriculture is longer lasting.

Not all the settlers were aristocrats. War veterans flocked to Kenya, lured by the promise of cheap land and labour. Boers arrived from South Africa and squatted illegally on native land. They weren't all successful, their animals threatened by tsetse fly and predators. Some of the new arrivals came for the hunting, others for the wildlife. Some, like Colonel Richard Meinertzhagen, came for both. The colonel, an officer in the King's African Rifles, was escaping from the over-civilized society of Britain, as he described it. He was an accomplished artist, ornithologist and amateur botanist who sent seeds to Kew. He was a contemporary of Grandfather Philip with whom he shared these talents as well as a German name. Coincidentally they were both in Palestine with Allenby during the First World War. Whether they met is uncertain, although Philip had a first edition of Meinertzhagen's diaries. Like many of the early settlers, Meinertzhagen was a law unto himself. He disapproved of the colonization of Kenya by Europeans, not because he sided with the Africans, but because he feared that the forests and game would disappear under cultivation. However, he did his bit to reduce the wildlife. One afternoon in between collecting ferns, seeds and bulbs, he managed to shoot a reedbuck, an oribi, two hartebeest and a pair of snipe, not all of it for the pot. He was famous as a slaughterer of beasts but he refused to shoot elephants. Later he was expelled from the colony in disgrace for shooting some members of the Nandi tribe with a machine gun.

No one would have fought over our patch on the edge of Nairobi. Nor was it tribal land. We were allocated a perfectly hideous little bungalow made of grey stone with a tiled roof. It sat like a pimple in a large dry plot surrounded by beds of red salvia. A mature fig tree provided shade. There were, too, lacy-leaved pepper trees with their pink seeds, clumps of bamboo and a lonely lemon tree, which,

Family bungalow in Nairobi

despite its anorexic appearance, produced fruit. The house was one
of four, all equally ugly, on a hill near the hospital where Clinton
worked. It had a sweeping view over the Athi Plains, dotted with
scrubby thorn trees and home to the Nairobi National Park. On a
clear day we could see Mount Kilimanjaro with its head of snow.
Colonial children who lived in the bush had more exotic lives than
those of us who lived in suburban Nairobi. They had unusual pets
like monkeys, bush babies or dik-dik (a tiny antelope), were best
friends with African children and could speak Kikuyu or Swahili like
a native. Our lives were quite ordinary: school, the club where we
played sports, visits to friends' houses. We had dogs, cats or rabbits.
But Grandfather Philip, who visited us on a safari, insisted on telling
everyone, including passengers at Westerham railway station, that
we had leopards and hyenas in our garden. People would stare at
us, expecting something more exciting than two children in their
school uniforms. We willed him to stop. What year was he living in?
Had he read how in 1910 Nairobi residents had complained about

giraffes and zebras ruining their gardens? We wouldn't have minded the odd giraffe in our garden. But we had fought bush fires and locust swarms on the hill below our house. We had eaten flying ants alive after tearing the wings off, and we could boast our very own Mau Mau neighbour, who, unknown to us, lived next door.

Our home was pokey. It had three small bedrooms, a bathroom, sitting room and dining room, kitchen and a porch-verandah. The servants' quarters were at the rear of the garden: three whitewashed rooms with high windows, an outhouse with a lavatory in the floor and a tap with water. We started with two servants, Impishi (cook) and Andrea the 'garden boy', a mature man in his thirties whose job included killing snakes and rescuing pets or retrieving us from trees. Every Christmas Andrea carefully wrapped up sugar cane stalks in newspaper and presented them to us on the day. There is nothing quite so good as sucking the sweetness out of a fresh stalk and spitting out a trail of pulp. Both Impishi and Andrea came recommended by other families. It was something of a tradition that when a family left, they found employment for their servants with other families. Later, with independence, this became more difficult as an African middle class grew up and wanted servants. Most of the servants we knew preferred to work for white families. Impishi and Andrea both received salaries as well as weekly rations of meat and vegetables. Andrea brought his family with him but Impishi lived on his own. Neither of our servants were a threat, neither belonged to the Kikuyu tribe. Andrea came from a small tribe who lived on the shores of Lake Victoria. Nevertheless, both had to be locked out of the house from sunset until the following morning. Clinton and Joan both slept with revolvers under their pillows. Joan was terrified of hers and frequently lost it. There would be mad panics; there were heavy fines for lost guns. There were restrictions on our freedom. You couldn't just go out for a walk, ride a horse or bicycle down the road. So we went everywhere by car. Clinton had been appointed senior consultant physician at the King George VI

Hospital (later the Kenyatta). Medical care was free to all but there were separate hospitals for Africans and Europeans. Clinton worked at both of them. He also helped set up the medical school, which trained African doctors and became one of Africa's best. Its research institutes in the 1960s became one of the world's foremost centres for tropical disease, this despite some colonial physicians' attempts to end the influence of Patrick Manson and concentrate on issues like heart disease, which was virtually unknown in Africa. This preservation of 'tropical medicine' was largely thanks to Clinton. Clinton never became as famous as his father or grandfather; he didn't court fame. He preferred doing research to ministering to patients. He did, however, make important contributions in the field of trypanosomiasis (sleeping sickness), where he discovered that the bushbuck was the reservoir for the disease. He discovered the African vectors of leishmaniasis – also known as kala-azar (a tiny sand fly), and usually fatal. Clinton was the first to try a leishmaniasis vaccine. Later he found that leishmaniasis was widespread in the Mediterranean. He studied little-known tanapox (a viral infection and nothing to do with smallpox) and histoplasmosis, a lung infection caused by inhaling fungal spores found in the soil and in bird and bat droppings. His research included marine typhus, plague, and leptospirosis (a bacterial disease), which is spread through the urine of infected animals, mainly rodents. He discovered that hyenas, jackals and wild dogs were reservoirs of hydatid disease (tapeworms). Wild pigs and carnivores were reservoirs of trichinosis (roundworms). Clinton believed in the use of field officers who could get out to the villages and fostered close relations between them and the hospital (these are now widely used). While these discoveries were not as dramatic as the discovery of malaria, these were serious and debilitating illnesses. It was always a bone of contention with Joan that Clinton didn't do private practice like many of the other consultants there. He could have done. He had the name, the knowledge and the credentials. It was well paid and we needed the money. Clinton didn't care about money, although he did care about not having enough. He had given up the promise of a good life in Britain, where he could have earned more, had a house in the Home Counties and had ridden to hounds. My brother and I thought that, like Meinertzhagen, he had escaped the 'civilized' pleasures of England. He had also escaped an over-bearing father and a life he no longer wanted. The standard of living in the Colonial Service was no better than at home, and in some cases worse, although there were compensations and the promise of a reasonable pension. Africa offered him the freedom to do his research without interference and to see interesting medical cases rather than examine retired colonials with malaria. He was awkward except in the areas where he excelled and unlike his father was no good at small talk. He cared little for social rules. He was like an overgrown schoolboy, bubbling with enthusiasm, always excited, pleased to be alive in this wonderful natural world he had discovered. As often as he could, he escaped into the bush to hunt for animals that might be reservoirs of parasites.

One of Clinton's favourite areas was Lake Turkana. This alkaline lake shaped like an arrowhead stretched up into Ethiopia through a lunar landscape dotted with craters. Not much grew here apart from a few douam palms and solitary acacias. This was an ancient land, as shown in the thirty-six-million-year-old basalt lava flows one kilometre deep. Here too was found the almost complete skeleton of teenage Turkana Boy, who lived 1.5 million years ago. More recent were the remains of a 10,000-year-old massacre of hunter-gatherers whose bodies bore wounds inflicted by obsidian arrowheads. Now it is inhabited by the Nilotic Turkana, an elegant people with ebony skin. But there are still wars for women and cattle. Whenever we heard the word 'war' in Kenya it always meant a tribal raid. In 1931 there had been several outbreaks of leishmaniasis in the region. When Clinton was serving in the army in 1941 an outbreak of kala-

Clinton taking bloods to check for parasites

azar, the most severe form of the disease, struck soldiers from the King's African Rifles. Leishmaniasis is carried by female sandflies and there was plenty of sand in Lake Turkana. Clinton returned there in the 1950s to do his research. He had special permits to hunt in protected areas and would stay some three or four weeks. Leaving for Turkana was always a drama. The jeeps would line up outside the hospital with all the kit, tents and food, medical equipment and, most important, paraffin fridges for the cold beer. Even then Turkana was as hot as hell. Travelling with Clinton were the drivers, the cooks, the trackers and a group of fellow-minded friends, including parasitologists and doctors and Clinton's African assistant Justice, all shaking with excitement. It was Justice who organized the expedition, who found the helpers and asked the chief's permission to take blood from the villagers. This was never a problem and what the chief decided, the tribe obeyed. The villagers were rewarded with a hot meal and a polaroid photo. Justice did rather better. Instead of a photo, he found a live young girl warming his bed.

As soon as camp was made, the cooks set to making bread in mud ovens and cooking the meat (shot for the pot) for supper. Afterwards everyone would sit around the camp fire drinking whisky and slagging off the politicians back home. All inhibitions vanished out there in the bush; all the prejudices arrived with the night insects and were openly expressed. No one went hungry when Clinton had his shotgun. As a family we lived on guinea fowl. Even freshly shot, the bird remained dry. Gordon, my brother, who had a gun since the age of eleven, often went on safari. He remembered the horror of going alone to the bush lavatory at night. "Don't worry," Clinton would say, "we'll keep the Land Rover lights on for you. Just make for them when you are finished." What if they failed?

On one occasion, my brother swam in Lake Turkana where there were crocodiles. Clinton positioned himself on the bank, quivering with excitement, his legs braced, his rifle loaded and pointed at the

Gordon on safari

water. It took a lot of skill and speed to shoot a croc, by which time the victim might well have been dragged underneath the water. The night hunts for hyenas (mainly for research) were equally dangerous. Hyenas are unattractive beasts like guard dogs from the underworld. Gordon, as the smallest person, was used to shoot the hyenas. Clinton would tie him to the spare tyre on the bonnet of the car and secure him with a rope to the passenger in the front seat. Then the Land Rover bounced off on the pot-holed tracks, searching for hyenas' eyes in the darkness. Hyenas not only look terrifying (they eat their prey alive), they are fast and difficult to kill. My brother sat there firing his gun into the night like a machine gun. Joan never found out. Women were rarely included on these trips. Betty, Joan's friend, was the exception. She had been brought up in Africa and knew the rules. She told rollicking tales of safari life. How she escaped a rhino charge by standing quite still as the animal approached and then, at the very last minute, jumping aside as the great beast thundered past. Or how a curious leopard surprised her crouching in the bush with her knickers down. Once when Clinton was alone in the bush he came across a native woman giving birth. He stopped to help and cut the cord. As soon as the child was born, the mother wrapped her newborn in a shawl around her chest, put her water can on her head and disappeared into the bush. Clinton tried to make amends to Joan for his long absences but his idea of a gift was unusual. One day he drew up outside the house and flung open the boot, sending sand everywhere. He grinned like a schoolboy.

"I've brought you a handbag."

There in the boot lay a five-foot monitor lizard, its clever hands folded delicately like an old lady drinking tea from a porcelain cup. Joan became weepy. This was not the welcome Clinton had expected.

"What's wrong?"

"Everything's wrong. You've killed a magnificent creature and for what?"

"For a handbag, dear. You could make more than one."

"I don't want it, do you hear me? I don't want it!"

We had last seen a monitor lizard sitting neatly in an acacia tree. It had turned its head to look at us when we stopped the car. Joan covered her eyes. Clinton looked confused. He didn't understand.

As a doctor, Clinton was treated with respect by the Africans, who were grateful for their treatment. However, some of Clinton's patients were beyond the help of Western medicine. When an African man in his thirties was carried into the hospital suffering from a mysterious ailment, Clinton was baffled. The patient lay in a coma.

"He's been cursed," said the African nurse.

Nonsense, thought Clinton.

"The witch doctor has put a spell on him. You cannot save him."

Within three days the patient was dead. There was nothing that could be done. This was beyond Clinton's expertise. Witch doctoring had not been taught at the London Hospital.

On my 10th birthday, my brother and I and our new friend, the boy next door, were sitting on the fence eating cake when we heard gut-wrenching screams. An African youth rushed past us hotly pursued by a man waving a panga (machete). Clinton rushed from the house clutching his gun, followed by Andrea our gardener. It was like a cowboy film, guns firing, feet pounding as the neighbours, black and white, joined in the stampede. The pursuer was caught. He had been trying to force his victim to take the Mau Mau oath. You never knew who might be a member of the Mau Mau. Even the most unlikely might have taken the oath, like my African friend next door. I met him one morning when I went to feed my rabbits and found a trail of ants pouring into the hutch. Inside was my buck, half dead, coated in black ants. "Siafu," said a voice. Soldier ants, known as siafu, were relentless in their search of prey. Nothing was safe in their path. There were even stories of babies found dead in their prams. We children used to pick up the ants on sticks, transfer them to our shorts and tear the bodies away, leaving the wriggling heads. The one with the most heads won the game. I picked up Benji by the ears and ran to the house and threw him into a bath full of cold water. The ants floated off. He survived. As I carried him back to his hutch, the man was still there, leaning over the fence.

"Charcoal," he drawled, "you need charcoal. You put it around his hut, top it up regularly, the ants will never get in."

I was sceptical, but it worked. No ants ever got into that hutch again. My new friend waited for me often in a small room he occupied in the servants' quarters next door. Since the house next door was empty, it seemed odd to have someone living in a room that looked like a chemists' shop, with shelves of pills and potions, bandages and the odd syringe. I thought nothing of it. I felt grown up drinking tea with a grown-up. He seemed to know a lot about us. A week later Joan told me that we had a Mau Mau general living next door who was in charge of procuring medical supplies. The police had been looking for him for some time. Had I noticed anything? I said nothing. This was not an adventure for grown-ups. But I was sorry to see him go. All that was left was an outhouse with empty shelves and shards of glass and no one to drink tea with.

If you wanted anything in Nairobi, you went to an Indian dukka which was an Aladdin's cave of treasures: silks, cashmere shawls, Persian rugs, jewellery, shoes, home goods, Indian furniture. Other dukkas sold fruit and veg neatly laid out in wooden sheds. Nothing was impossible. If it wasn't on display, the shopkeepers would find it for you. The Indians were marvellous retailers. Joan would produce a design for our clothes and have them run up by an Indian tailor on his Singer sewing machine. As we walked down the street in the bazaar all we could hear was the gossipy clickety-clack of the pedal sewing machines. Nairobi was not a pretty town; it was put up in a hurry. But its wide avenues lined with jacarandas and tree-covered islands for the traffic police softened the effect of impermanence. There were no coffee shops despite Kenya being a major producer of coffee, and few restaurants. Dinners were usually in hotels, although we never ate out. There was a theatre, a university (for all races) and a good museum packed with artefacts collected by the Leakey family. Clinton had a wide network of friends, school friends, university friends, hospital friends, family friends, sporting friends, who covered the globe. On our ship voyages, we had 'guides' in every port. One friend in Kenya had a coffee farm in the highlands. This involved a long drive through the Rift Valley. The road climbed the escarpment in steep hairpin bends where the cars slowed down but you never lingered to look at the view. The Mau Mau had mastered the trick of dropping rocks onto the cars below. My brother and I were terrified. "Faster, Dad," we'd beg. Clinton ignored us. But we didn't trust his judgement. After all, hadn't he exposed us to a charging elephant in the Nairobi National Park? He had told us, as he assembled his camera and tripod, that it was just for show and roared with laughter when we tried to hide under the back seat. When the elephant came for us, Clinton barely had the time to get back into the car, turn on the ignition and drive off. Although elephants have terrible eyesight and poor hearing, they have a heightened sense of smell. They had been known to search out every person in an upturned car. We had friends who had crawled out and got away. Fortunately the wind was in the right direction and the elephant didn't smell them.

The Rift Valley road was treacherous enough without the threat of falling rocks but the rutted track to the coffee farm worried Clinton and Joan far more. They argued fiercely as the trees closed in on us. Joan wanted to turn back. What if we got stuck? It was a relief to reach the farm, with its perfect lawns and clipped hedges, a small slice of England in an alien environment. Two parents, four children, an elderly grandfather and a mature English nanny lived in the sprawling old house. Once a month, the parents drove to the theatre in Nairobi, leaving the children on the farm with the old couple. They stayed the night in a hotel and returned the next day. One night, the Mau Mau crept out of the forest. The elderly grandfather picked up the story.

"They charged out of the forest firing. We couldn't see how many there were. I went out with my shotgun and fired blindly in the dark. One threw a flare at the thatch but it failed to catch. I did several rounds just to be sure. Nanny here loaded the guns. They must have thought there were more of us because they fled."

In the morning, three bodies were found on the lawn.

We left at tea time, before it got dark. We weren't sorry to go. As we crawled along the track, hoping that the car wouldn't break down, Joan sat with lips pursed in disapproval.

"What if those children had been killed?"

This 'can do' attitude was typical of the settlers. They sat it out on their farms with their guns at the ready. Some of them formed their own patrols but the farms were isolated and far from neighbours. We learnt later that our friends had been caught in an ambush one night. They managed to escape. Our main danger in Nairobi were the pole fishers, who would stuff their poles through the bars on the windows. We never heard them. The first we knew was when we woke up without blankets. Clinton and Joan didn't worry too much about the Mau Mau. They carried on as normal. When they went to cocktail parties, they left us in the car outside. Their only advice was to lock ourselves in. Fortunately these were quiet suburbs with no loiterers.

Jomo Kenyatta had been put under house arrest outside Nairobi and supplied with enough whisky to kill an elephant. Doctors visited him regularly but his health remained good. His personal physician, a garrulous Welshman, was a friend of Clinton's. They got on famously, drinking their way through the stores of whisky. Jomo played a waiting game as he had all his life. He had been educated at a mission school followed by university in Moscow, then University College London and the London School of Economics, where he obtained a degree in anthropology. He was a skillful politician and writer. In 1938 he published his study of his Kikuyu tribe, *Facing Mount Kenya*, with a preface by Malinowski.

There were wilder candidates for the Mau Mau leadership, like Dedan Kimathi, who led the struggle from 1950 until his execution by the British in 1957. Jomo wasn't one of his fans. In 1952, Kenyatta was arrested and accused of masterminding the Mau Mau (for which there was no evidence). He was imprisoned until 1959 and put under house arrest until 1961. He became first prime minister and then president until 1978. There were accusations of favouring his own tribe the Kikuyu (the Mau Mau was predominantly Kikuyu) and rumours of corruption. But he managed to keep the peace between the tribes, the whites and the Asians. Later when stories emerged about torture, it seemed unbelievable. We British didn't do that kind of thing, did we? Or did we get others to do our dirty work? There was bitter feeling on both sides. Africans who had refused the oath had been tortured. They had seen their families murdered. There were twenty-seven different tribes in Kenya and not all fans of the Kikuyu. Some guards took their revenge. No one seemed to know anything about this. The prisons were in distant places off the radar. Still, it was a shock when, years later, the truth was revealed, when archives went missing, and to discover how many witnesses had kept their lips sealed. Later we learnt the truth from those who had been there. But we children thought that the Africans liked us (some did). Before we left Kenya, my brother and I were sitting in our car in a petrol station when an African banged on our window. We were terrified until he grinned.

"Dr Manson-Bahr's children? He is a good man. You can stay."

When we told Clinton, he laughed.

"He'll change his mind tomorrow."

The East African coast was a different country, warm, tropical, easy-going and free of the Mau Mau. It had a long and settled past going back over 1,000 years as part of the Moslem Swahili culture. Its people, a mixture of Arab and African, were the result of years of slave

The singing ferry at Kilifi

trading by the Arabs, which continued along this coast well into the 20th century. Porcelain shards from 14th century China found in the ruins of the mediaeval towns showed wide trading links. One such town was 12th century Gedi. When we visited, Clinton would rush to peer down into the wells, wondering what ancient parasites might be hidden in the silt. He was less interested in the Chinese coins and porcelain. It was a long and dirty journey to the sea, with a night spent en route and a day at Tsavo Park, which teemed with game. We stopped often as the animals strolled across the road. There were no predatory safari vehicles chasing them. We always arrived covered in red dust. As we dropped down from the highlands the climate became hot and humid. Ravenous mosquitoes gathered to feast. Ant castles and baobab trees colonized the earth. We called them upside-down trees. They looked as if they might have shared their territory with dinosaurs. There are many legends about them. My favourite said that each baobab at the coast marked the grave of a Portuguese sailor buried with a seed pod in his hand. Baobabs can live for up to 500 years. Their thick cork-like bark is fire resistant and can be used for cloth and rope. Their pods contain an edible pulp known as 'monkey bread', useful in famines and not just for monkeys. We usually bypassed Mombasa in favour of Malindi further up the coast. It was reached by a ferry that carried only two cars at a time and was pulled across on chains by a chorus of Africans. We called it 'the singing ferry'. Our borrowed cottages were on the beach. Some had no electric light. A major risk was the night visit to the outdoor lavatory. We always went in pairs. Shoes had to be worn (after being inspected for scorpions, who also liked to hide underneath the lavatory seat). You could smell the long drop from way off. While one went in, the other waited outside with the torch. You could tell how full the hole was by how long it took for our deposits to drop. We would count and then rush back before something sinister might find us. In the morning, in full sun, there was nothing sinister as we walked to the beach fringed by silver casuarina trees, followed by Joan in her huge sun hat and carrying her basket of towels – shadowed by Clinton marching into the sea with his fins and harpoon gun. We would sit on the sand and wait for the cry.

"It's huge!"

When the harpoon emerged, the fish at the end was no bigger than a plum. The balloon fish had blown itself up to escape Clinton's predations. It happened every time. The beach was usually deserted except for one or two fishermen and women from the local Giriama tribe. Once we brought Andrea, our servant, with us. He had never seen the sea, but what terrified him most were the bare-breasted Giriama women in their wide grass skirts. Now Malindi is a major centre of tourism. When Clinton went back some years later he met an old doctor friend who had a clinic there. He told Clinton that business had never been better. The tourists stayed just long enough to develop symptoms of gonorrhoea.

Christmas and Easter were spent with Joan's friend Betty in Kericho on a tea estate owned by Brooke Bond and managed by her husband. The job came with an 'English' cottage in the middle of a forest clearing. Kericho was home to the Kipsigis tribe – famous runners and winners in the Olympics. At 8,000 feet it was cool and wet, the perfect climate for tea. We children liked to stand on the edge of the forest and listen to the black and white colobus monkeys chattering in the tree canopy, but we weren't allowed in without a minder, who carried a bow and arrow to shoot the rabid jackals. We liked our minder. Not only was his shot accurate, but he was elegant, his skin as shiny black as if he had been polished. We made friends too with the seven-year-old Duck Boy, who taught us how to make a bow and arrows and roared with laughter when we were unable even to tense the bow string. In spring Betty's garden was a haven of primroses and daffodils. We would get up early in the morning and run outside to see the dew glistening on the lawn. At Christmas we had carol singing, a tree, parties, our own nativity play and a log fire.

And then when I was twelve and my brother nine, our idyll ended with an announcement that my brother and I were going to boarding school in England.

Betty's English cottage in Kericho

EXILE IN THE HOME COUNTRY

1959–1961

School days – author bottom row, fourth from left

There had been no hints that life would change. We were both happy at our schools. Mine was a convent, a fragment of Spain in Africa, its Moorish courtyard dominated by a marble statue of the Virgin Mary. I liked the peace. I liked the coffee fields that surrounded us. I liked the swish of the sisters' skirts as they swept the floors and I curtseyed like a ballet dancer whenever they passed. I collected holy pictures with gold borders and cerulean madonnas and swapped them like stamps. We Protestants were tolerated but there was a feeling that we might not be first in the queue for heaven. Bells separated the days into class and prayers. Now my brother and I were being exiled to a country we had visited infrequently but was called 'home'.

The previous year, 1954, Kenya had suffered a severe polio epidemic. It picked out the young and healthy. Teenagers at our brother school who had been training hard for a cycle race suffered particularly badly. One was paralyzed for life. The King George Hospital set up an ICU unit in a converted cottage. Like during Covid, the staff, including Clinton, wore full PPE. The survival rate was pushed up by the use of the Both respirator – known as the iron lung – which was made in William Morris's car factory in Oxford and sent free to Commonwealth countries. It looked like a chrysalis on a trolley with two small windows and was airtight. The patient was squashed inside as air was pumped in mechanically to keep their lungs working. We hardly saw Clinton during this time. Some nights he stayed in the ICU unit; all the doctors took turns. When the power failed, as it sometimes did, they had to transfer everything to the generators. When Clinton came home, Joan would run a bath, pour in the Dettol and scrub him. None of us got polio but when we went shopping in Nairobi we were treated like lepers. When the Salk vaccine came out in 1957, my brother and I were among the first children to be vaccinated. The epidemic had come as a shock. Perhaps it focused Clinton's mind on the future. There was always, for colonial children, the problem of where to fit in.

"Who will want you here?" said Clinton. "You will always be an outsider."

I was removed from the convent and sent to a crammer run by Major H Massey-Blomfield, a bandy-legged relic of the Indian Cavalry who looked like Don Quixote. There were twelve of us in his class, only two of us girls. Our trick was to make the major pronounce 'petite poire' in French lessons and watch his false teeth clatter to the ground. We all passed. My brother's choice of school was easy. Sons went to their father's and their grandfather's school regardless of whether it was good or not. My brother's school was in Westgate-on-Sea, not even nicely provincial, and run by a headmaster who liked beating his pupils' bare buttocks. My school was altogether more civilized. It was a Church of England foundation in one of the more pleasant small cities in England. Clinton and Joan knew nothing about it other than people who knew people who knew people who knew girls who had gone there. There was, however, a respite before the storm. As a treat before we left Kenya, Clinton took us to Buffalo Springs near the one-horse town of Isiolo in Northern Kenya, which he knew from his war-time days driving up to Ethiopia. The country was dry, semi-arid plains of lava flows, home to pastoralists like the Turkhana, the Boran and the Samburu, all nomads who had managed to retain their identity in a world that had less and less space for them. Stubborn thorn trees clung to the dust-blown soil around the spring. We swam through the clear water to the edge of the giant cavern behind the swimming hole where turtles stared back at us. I photographed it with my mind for the future. We thought we were alone but it is the law of such places that whenever you want to have a pee, several people turn up and ask for money. These Samburu goat herders were not after money. They crouched on their haunches by the side of the pool, cleaning their teeth with twigs from the toothbrush tree that grew nearby. When I emerged from the water in my tight costume, they told Clinton in Swahili that it was time I married. Clinton laughed and asked how many goats I was worth. The herders scrutinized me carefully. I was small for my age. I don't remember their answer but I do remember that sudden unpleasant jolt into adulthood. Their searching stares unsettled me. I wanted to hide in my shell like the turtles swimming beneath me in the springs. Joan had taken me aside to warn me of bodily changes. She spoke in code.

"What changes, Mum?"

"You'll become a woman."

I was none the wiser. In today's world it is impossible to imagine a more naïve twelve-year-old but we lived far from happening places. We were out of touch. Joan never discussed such things and there was no social media. Our news came from the BBC and the airmail edition of *The Daily Telegraph*, which was always out of date.

"Don't let anyone touch you."

"Touch me where?"

Joan got flustered.

"Anywhere."

And that was the extent of my sexual briefing. I was soon put out of my misery at school in England by girls who knew everything there was to know and seemed perfectly comfortable with it.

Back we went on the boat down the East Coast, stopping off in South Africa to see Joan's relatives. They were aghast at our plans. "We have good schools here," they insisted. And they did. And they would have looked after us. They were a tightly knit group, all Scots and proud of it. My uncle considered himself the patriarch of the tribe to which we all belonged. They had all prospered in South Africa.

But Clinton didn't want us to become South African, so it had to be the 'home' country. The journey was a brief happy moment before 'growing up'. I made a friend on the boat going to school in the same county. We roamed the ship, swimming, playing, enjoying our last Crossing the Line ceremony, jumping over and over again off the diving board into Neptune's hairy arms, which gripped us just a little too tightly.

Clinton rented a cheap basement flat in Bayswater smelling of boiled cabbage. We went on outings to the school uniform shop. The salesman knew everything about colonial children, having provided clothes for most schools in the Empire. Drab scratchy tweeds and flannels hung over every rail in the shop. He was a bit sniffy about schools; his expression would magically change if Eton or Winchester were mentioned. My brother's school, Wellington House at Westgate-on-Sea, didn't register at all. In between visits to the store, my brother and I would stare out of the window at the trees in Hyde Park and long for home. At weekends we drove to Kent to visit Grandfather Philip. By now he had remarried. His new wife had been the secretary at his Harley Street practice. Molly, whom we children called Milly-Molly-Mandy, was a stick-thin woman whose main love-interest was her sickly dog. But she was more exciting than she looked. Rumour was that she had spread her favours throughout the consultants. By marrying Philip she gained financial security and a title but this did not include taking on the family. Philip had been caught on the hop when the national press descended one weekend to interview him when Molly was staying over. He had inherited a substantial property from his Blessig uncle but had turned it down, not wanting to be bothered with the running of an estate. It was sold, the proceeds divided and he remained happily in his cottage. The gardens were recognizably the same, cared for by a younger Charlie. Horses still roamed the fields. The John Peel musical mug was still there in the porch, just as I had left it. Philip's watercolours covered the walls. Only the mistress of the house had changed.

Philip lecturing

"I have everything I need," Philip told the journalists, as they photographed him with Molly and the dogs, "my horse, my dog and my wife" – in that order. It was in all the papers, so he had to make an honest woman of her. We never felt welcome. Milly-Molly considered us a nuisance and Philip was always too busy. We knew he was famous, so we made allowances. We stayed some of the time with our aunt Louise, who had been sent back from Germany during the war. And then in September, duly attired in our uniforms, hats, socks, ties, shoes and accompanied by large black trunks, we were taken to our respective schools and Clinton and Joan flew back to Kenya. Joan had mixed feelings about the whole process. For Clinton, boarding school was part of his culture. He wanted his children to have an education to prepare them for life in a changing world, although sometimes the schools seemed more like training colleges for the Empire. This changed when Suez erupted in 1956; we were all ordered to assemble in the school hall. Our headmistress gave us a serious talk. I remember the gravity of her words and feeling that something was changing forever. It was another nail in the coffin of the Empire.

It was difficult for colonial wives to know how best to deal with their children. Did they put their husband or their children first? Some ended up losing both. Many 'abandoned' husbands found solace with their bridge partners. Joan seemed particularly concerned about these risks. She knew several women who had returned to divorce. She guarded Clinton carefully, although he was too lazy to take on another woman; his research was far more important. But it was equally difficult for the relatives back home. They hadn't signed on for extra children. We had three aunts and spent half-terms with them. But for longer holidays it was a big demand. One aunt was single and worked as a nurse. The other two had their own families and, in one case, marital problems and certainly didn't need us. My favourite uncle was a surgeon in Salisbury. When he worked in Winchester he would often turn up unexpectedly to check on me. Once he found me ill with flu, put me in the car and carried me away, like a knight in shining armour. His house was a mini paradise nestled on the edge of beech woods above the River Avon. I had my own small room tucked under the eaves, where I lay at night listening to the gurgling of the water tank. I envied my cousins for living there. I envied them too for their grandmother who lived nearby and who slipped two shillings into my pocket every time I visited.

My school was a modern red-brick building on the edge of Winchester, surrounded by fields of grass and wheat. It was and is an excellent school but in the 1950s such schools were not the comfortable establishments they are today. Baths that were rationed, short hair, shared dormitories and a regime of church and sport. Sport meant team games, running around in brief brown shorts waving a ball in a net and trying not to drop it. Even swimming was hard core, in a concrete pool of freezing water. We were so cold we couldn't do up our bra straps. In summer, when the fields were a carpet of wild flowers, we played cricket. Although those fields looked picturesque, the grass released its pollen in the summer, usually at exam time. Hayfever wasn't considered a proper ailment, and there were no antihistamines to treat it. It was something to be endured and another reason to think that colonials were inherently unhealthy. But swollen, weeping eyes, a tight chest and blocked nose didn't help study.

I had chosen to board in an Edwardian house four miles from school. This meant cycling in all weathers twice a day, which I enjoyed. The house had a pretty garden with a lawn tennis court but inside it was dingy and cold. There was little heating. The housemistress had 'favourites'. Few colonials made this list. My friend Sylvia from Calcutta was always in trouble. One day she locked herself into her dormitory and placed all six beds against the door and refused to emerge. The negotiations took some time. Sylvia became a respected geriatrician. I escaped into my mind. I invented characters that I drew (later in life I earned my living as a card designer). Piano was another diversion. You could always be alone in the practice room.

The Easter holidays were always a problem for my brother and me. We felt like unwanted refugees. Had our grandmother been alive, things might have been different. Most colonial children had grandparents who cared. Our aunt Patricia, born in Fiji, had us to stay the first year. She did all the things a mother should do. She sorted our clothes, took us to the dentist, bought our bikes. With a large house, a husband and four children, she didn't need two more. She looked after us well and yet we felt in the way. It wasn't our home. The rules were different in England. There was the feeling that colonial children were a bit 'bush'. My uncle fondly called me Jungle Wallah because I hated wearing shoes. Yet it was safer to run barefoot in England than in Kenya, where jiggers were prevalent. Jiggers are tiny sand fleas that burrow under the skin of the foot and lay their eggs. These result in painful and itchy lesions. You have to extract the jigger before the eggs develop. There were no such dangers in Kent.

We missed everything about home. We missed the sun. We missed our dog. We missed the tree house in the bamboo groves where the puff adders lurked. We missed our cook, whose meals were hit and miss. Once, in the presence of a distinguished visiting doctor whose hands trembled as he took his gravy (he had Parkinson's), Andrea dropped the gravy boat and fled screaming out of the house to escape the evil spirits. My aunt had a cook who did not believe in evil spirits. You had to eat everything on your plate and if you left bits on the side you received a lecture about the starving children in Africa. Occasionally we visited Grandfather Philip for tea and sometimes he rode over to us on his hunter Merrymac.

After that first Easter with our aunt, Joan tried to find somewhere else for us to stay. Through the Chinese whispers of friends she found a holiday home near Chagford in Devon. Sandy Park is still there, although no longer a home for abandoned children. The owner had been a concert pianist in her youth and set up the business for her retirement. Now she was too old to deal with the mixed bag of children in her care ranging in age from three to fifteen. The three-year-old had been dumped at eighteen months while her parents explored the Amazon and was still there eighteen months later. Perhaps they had met the same fate as Tony in Evelyn Waugh's *A Handful of Dust*, given the Sisyphean task of reading Dickens aloud to a local chief every day for the rest of their lives.

There were games and days filled with activities. My brother and I saved our pocket money and walked every morning to the hotel by the bridge and drank coffee. You could read the papers too. We made the cups last.

"Do you think Mum and Dad are missing us? I even miss kidneys on toast like Andrea cooked for us," said my brother wistfully. We laughed; it was Andrea's signature dish.

Every Wednesday we were taken to the movies and there were walks on the moor. On one hot day while looking for a Saxon wall that none of us wanted to see, we hid in the heather – one minute there, the next gone – like an Exmoor version of *Picnic at Hanging Rock*. I don't remember how long we lay there, but long enough for the park rangers to be called out to search for us. My brother and I were told never to return. The four weeks passed all too slowly and it was a relief to go back to school, where everyone was boasting about their holidays at home.

The next year we lodged at a vicarage in Wadebridge in Cornwall, a beautiful house with a view over the Camel Estuary. It came with the vicar and his family. It was a shock to find the vicar's family short of cash, which is why they took us in. We had never gone hungry. This family lived leanly: high tea was one sardine, half a hard-boiled egg, bread and a lettuce leaf all eaten in silence. If anyone needed fattening up it was the vicarage children, who were thinner and more anaemic than any colonial. "They need food like the children in Africa," whispered my brother. We were both constantly hungry. We pooled our pocket money and stocked up on tins of pilchards, which we stored under our beds. With their jumble-sale clothes and free vegetables from the local squire's garden, the family sorely felt their lack of money. They made up for it on Sunday when the whole day was spent in church and the vicar wove his slights and disappointments into his sermons, venting his anger at the dramatic moments. He had wanted to train as a doctor and felt constantly cheated. Whether he shared some of the feelings against colonials, we didn't know, but we were guests for the money and my mother paid over the odds in the hope that at last she had found somewhere pleasant. The letters she received from us could not have helped.

My South African uncle and aunt came every year and took me out to lunch. Our parents never turned up. My brother was adopted by the family of his best friend, colonials like us now settled in Britain. They, and others, thought our parents negligent and said so openly. But it was difficult for Joan. She had lacked a mother in her young years and must have thought herself a nuisance as she was passed like a parcel around the family. She gave in to Clinton.

Besides, her children were getting the education she lacked. Despite her difficult childhood, she never expressed resentment; she was always cheerful, telling us never to complain. She hated moaners. Still, my brother felt very alone when he took and failed his A levels, which meant he wouldn't get into medical school. FIND A CRAMMER, wrote Clinton in bold letters in a blue airmail letter. My brother was seventeen. The best crammers were full. His future hung in the balance. Somehow, he managed to get himself onto an A-level conversion course run by St Thomas's Medical School for graduates wanting to become doctors. It helped that the dean was a friend of Grandfather Philip. After this we milked Philip's name for all it was worth. It did us well. It was our only legacy from him.

One year I returned late to school and took a train to Winchester. I wore my new fur-lined boots that my aunt had given me. I was so exhausted that I fell asleep in the train and ended up in Bognor Regis. It could have been Kurdistan, so little did I know of English geography. In those days the trains had framed maps of the journey fixed behind the seats. This proved helpful to foreigners like me. I saw I was way off course. I manhandled my trunk and changed trains. My unexpectedly late arrival at school failed to elicit sympathy. Mrs Ruston could only stare at my boots.

"And what are those?"

"Boots."

"They are not allowed at school."

"It doesn't say anywhere they are forbidden."

"Don't be insolent. You are only a junior. They will be confiscated and returned to you at the end of term."

I thought it unreasonable. Rules were only worth obeying if they were fair. Even my youngest aunt, Mary, who sorted out all the mistakes, declared that dealing with Mrs Ruston was so stressful she reached for the bottle when she got home. Once, when she was served tea by the matron, they were both so jittery that they forgot to put the tea leaves in the pot. I felt such a sense of grievance. I resolved never to co-operate. I would just do enough to get by, nothing more, nothing less. I had three years left before I could leave. First there was a rite of passage. Confirmation was expected; we were a church school. Although the elderly canon pointed out that it was not too late to change one's mind, no one spoke up. On the other hand, there were compensations: a service in Winchester Cathedral shared with Winchester College boys, a day out from school, presents and visits from relatives. The downside was that now we had to go to church twice on Sundays. Early morning communion didn't count. Still, there were pleasures in Winchester that were missing in Kenya. Music was one, such as in Winchester Cathedral when the organ fired up and blasted us all to Heaven. Nairobi Cathedral couldn't compete with that. And there was always in England the freedom to roam, the walks over the downs. But best of all was the end of the summer term when we would gather in the house on the last night and sing gaudy, an anthem to student life. "*Gaudeamus igitur*," we would bellow, without understanding the words (let us rejoice), knowing that we were going home the very next day.

One year Grandpa Philip and Milly-Molly-Mandy escorted us to the airport.

Milly-Molly's thin lips tightened, poised to say something momentous.

"Now, drink your milk and empty your bowels regularly."

My brother and I tried not to giggle. Could Milly-Molly possibly have bowels? She seemed so scrawny with nothing to pass. Travelling to Nairobi was a twenty-four-hour journey in a propeller plane, an Argonaut – London to Nairobi with four stops where we had to get out at the airports while the plane re-fuelled. Rome, Benghazi, heat and sticky lemonade. Khartoum, more heat and even stickier lemonade. We were always excited to see the plane waiting for us on the tarmac with its initials B.O.A.C. proudly painted on the side waiting to take us to the promised land. When we stepped inside we were surrounded by children like ourselves. The planes seemed huge but were really quite small. They were known as 'lollipop specials', for they were full of unaccompanied children with luggage labels tied onto their buttons with name, age and address. Some were very young, six or seven. This was only made possible with the help of 'aunties', young women appointed to look after us. We became members of the BOAC Junior Jet Club and were given a book like a pilot's log. Its elegant blue and gold cover matched our 'wings', a blue and gold enamel badge. We wore these proudly. The pilot filled in the logbook recording our flights. When the total added up we gained special privileges. My brother's plane was once grounded in Cairo. The children on board were all put up in a hotel and taken by the aunties to see the pyramids. Being a stewardess in those days was seen as a glamorous job and a chance to see the world with long stop-overs. When that plane door shut and the engines revved up we felt like escaping prisoners. The plane flew over the Sahara as the sun was rising, casting shadows over the vast empty landscape beneath us. After neat little patchwork England with its fields and trees and spreading clusters of towns, this was a reminder that not all the world had been tamed. Our last stop was Entebbe in Uganda. By now we were deafened by the noise of the engines, although twenty-four hours of tinnitus seemed a price worth paying. At Nairobi we touched down on the Athi plain at Embakasi airport (now Jomo Kenyatta International). We were lucky to have two flights a year since flying in the 50s and 60s was expensive. The Colonial Office paid for one flight home annually for each of us and Joan went to work in the local tax office for a friendly Sikh to cover extra journeys. I too worked for Mr Singh in my holidays, where I was given the filing.

By now, Joan, ground down by my moaning, enrolled me in a school in Nairobi. My parents chose the Kenya Girls' High School, a government school for white girls just outside Nairobi.

Despite living locally, I boarded. We had our own cubicles; we could shower every day and even wash our hair when we wanted. Sports were fun on the 100-acre campus and the weather was kind. We had a large open-air swimming pool, open-air theatre and tennis courts set in wonderful grounds with bougainvillea and flame trees. The nickname for the school was 'the boma'. A boma was where cattle were kept. This was supposedly because we all had large backsides. My friend Ruth, later to study medicine at University College London, was head of Curie House (the ten houses were named after famous European women), where I boarded. In 1975 the Kenya government took over the school and admitted African and Asian girls. The house names were changed to the names of African rivers. During the holidays we played tennis and swam at the club, that nucleus of colonial life. We spent weeks at the coast. Things had moved on. There were night clubs and boys. But the beaches were still empty apart from the fishermen casting their nets on the ocean side of the reef. Social life was changing too. One day Clinton suggested inviting some of his students to dinner at our home. Joan was speechless.

"They are Africans, Clinton."

"They are educated men, dear."

By the standards of the time Joan would not have been considered racist. Most white memsahibs would have felt the same. They would have defended themselves fiercely, saying that the Africans too would have felt uncomfortable. Joan never maltreated people because of their race. She was always polite, always considerate. She treated her African servants properly but never considered them her equals. This was equally true in English country houses where the 'below stairs' staff were not treated as equals. The truth was that Joan felt threatened by clever people, especially clever Africans. Her own education had been inadequate. She knew her limitations. The empire had given her status as a white memsahib and she protected it fiercely. When a doctor student of Clinton's invited my parents to their wedding, I went instead of Joan. It wasn't a cocktail party where everyone mumbled politely. It was noisy and exuberant with dancing and laughter.

The first solid hint of change came in 1960 when the Belgian Congo became independent under the rule of Patrice Lumumba. This resulted in a flood of refugees escaping to Kenya and the surrounding countries. Our school was designated a hostel for refugee women. We older girls acted as hosts, shocked by the stories we heard. Even the nuns were raped. We saw the terror in the eyes of the mixed-race women who had no future in a new African Congo and nowhere else to go. This was happening in our own back yard. Now the reality of the political situation hit. Suddenly life felt precarious. In February that year, Harold Macmillan had made his famous 'Winds of Change' speech to the South African parliament in Cape Town. It shocked the South Africans and caused an outcry in Kenya. Joan considered the prime minister a traitor.

"The wind of change is blowing through this continent. Whether we like it or not, this growth of national consciousness is a political fact."

Joan wanted to move to South Africa. Betty and Colin were moving to Zimbabwe to set up a safari company. Other friends were emigrating to Australia and New Zealand. But Clinton was planning further afield. The World Health Organization had offered him a job. It meant travel and a better income, tax free too. But I was a problem. Clinton and Joan were reluctant to leave me behind in Kenya while they were travelling. I wanted to stay. I was in the A stream and in line to take exams for Oxbridge. I could live with Ruth's family. Joan didn't approve. Looks mattered, not brains. She argued with Clinton.

"She'll get married."

Clinton sighed.

"Have you heard of death and divorce, dear?"

Joan won. And so it was decided, I would go to school in Switzerland. They would write to me from wherever Clinton was working. They would return to Kenya before moving on again. After that who knew where we would end up, only that it wouldn't be England. Clinton was in no hurry to return 'home'. He was adamant there was no future in Africa. Joan insisted it would see us out. And so, at the end of the academic year, I boarded a new jet plane and flew to Switzerland, where I would stay for two years. After all, it was just another move to a different continent, which wasn't in the pink zone in the Atlas and had the wrong kind of stamps.

Europe looked appealing as our train wound its way around the lake to Lausanne. It was autumn, the trees were turning and the pickers were out in the vineyards. Snow had already dusted the mountains. "Les Dents du Midi," said the stern Scottish lady who had come to collect me from the airport. The mountain did indeed resemble a giant molar. The train skirted past villas with lawns running down to the shore. The water was choppy like a sea but I knew from geography lessons that this was the outflow of the Rhone Glacier on its journey to the Mediterranean. A crowded ferry was making its way across to the French side. Sailing boats bobbed in the shallows. The school occupied two large villas in a residential tree-lined street on a hill above the lake. Both were painted white, with green shutters, and were connected by a covered bridge. They had towers, mansard windows and decorative little orbs on the roof like those on alpine churches. The gravel crunched under my feet. An outsize front door under a rococo plaster wreath led into a hall with a black and white marble floor where an elegant old lady greeted me. She looked nothing like a head mistress.

"Welcome to Brillantmont, Elizabeth. You don't look a bit like your aunts."

This was a compliment. My aunts who had attended the same

school were sporty and had legs to match. Joan always said they had ankles like tree trunks, which was almost as bad as having crooked teeth. Beyond the hall was the dining room with windows stretching from ceiling to floor, giving a view across the lake to France. Tables were set for dinner with silver and linen. The food was French and there were four courses: soup, main, desert and cheese. This really was like a hotel. Mind you, I hadn't stayed in many hotels. We shared three to a room, with chintz curtains, central heating and beds with goose-down duvets. My fellow pupils came from all over the world. I lacked their sophistication and their well-cut clothes – those girls didn't go to Indian tailors. I vowed to save my pocket money and up my game. The classes were small; there were only ten or twelve of us and all our lessons were in French. I no longer had to get up early in the morning for lacrosse practice, although a jog before breakfast was encouraged. This was a serious school. Many of its students were trying for university. They could sit exams for Oxbridge, the Sorbonne, the American colleges or the local *ecoles*. In our free time we could go to concerts and exhibitions, stroll in the park and ride horses along the shore. *I could live here*, I thought, as I looked at the Dents du Midi every morning, checking whether it had snowed in the night, which meant a ski outing. Our ski teacher, a grave-digger in summer, was suitably aged and deemed safe with school girls.

"Young ladies," he used to say as he placed a leaf between our knees, "ski like virgins." He winked. "And keep your legs together." And we did.

Letters came from Joan and Clinton, from Russia, Iran, Uzbekistan. During my second year, Joan wrote to tell me that I would be going to university in America, where Clinton had been offered a position as professor of tropical medicine at a college in the Deep South. I sat my American college boards in Lausanne, answering questions by ticking boxes and completing an essay. 'Are there heroes in the modern world?' I also had to pass police questioning, confirming that I wasn't a communist or a criminal and nor did I run a brothel. I had mixed feelings about moving again. The only Americans I knew were some of my fellow pupils who had steady boyfriends and smoked behind the tennis courts. Perhaps I could stay in Switzerland. I felt at home there. It didn't have the drama of Africa with the big skies and open landscapes that could dwarf a human. It had cows with bells instead of wild animals. It had history. It had castles on crests. It had art galleries, shops and cafes. It was nicely bourgeois and everything worked. It was *civilized*. But my plane ticket was booked. My fate was sealed. I emerged a fully-fledged European in a chic new coat and moved across the Atlantic to yet another continent: America.

AMERICA NORTH AND SOUTH

1962–1965

Students at the National University of Mexico dressed as queens for a bullfight, with their cowboy bullfighter Rancho Aguilar – the author is second from left

We arrived in Louisiana during a hot and steamy August. The hurricane season was on its way. The civil rights movement was in full swing. We sat in a box-like apartment, clinging to the air-conditioning. We had travelled to New York on the *Queen Mary*, dropping to second class since the Colonial Office was no longer paying our passage. We had been exiled from our comfortable bubble where we were known and respected, and catapulted into the real world. It was a shock. Louisiana wasn't our first choice. But we were lucky. New Orleans was one of the more interesting cities in America and Tulane one of its best colleges and I had been offered a free place. I entered college as a sophomore, a second-year student, since my British-European education had put me a year ahead of the American freshers. My brother only came for the school holidays. If he remained with us he risked being called up to fight in Vietnam despite not being an American citizen.

New Orleans didn't look at all New World, with its French and Spanish colonial buildings, its antebellum homes, its street cars and paddle steamers that churned their way up and down the mighty Mississippi. You could be forgiven for thinking yourself in a scene from *Gone with the Wind* if you stood at the port watching the porters sweating as they laboured in the sun. The people too seemed rather old-fashioned. Their slow southern accent was hypnotic. When we could face the heat, we explored the old French Quarter, which was as charming as the tourist brochures proclaimed, its wrought-iron balconies draped with purple bougainvillea. Most buildings were late 18th century, from when the city was under French rule. In

1803 the United States bought Louisiana from Napoleon, who was badly in need of money. We wandered through Jackson Square and admired the triple-steepled St Louis Cathedral and the large statue of General Jackson on his horse. Jackson had led the victory over the British in the Battle of New Orleans in 1815. This city, with its French and Spanish heritage, was founded in 1718 and built on a rise above the swamps. It had always been vulnerable to flooding. The first levees were built by the French in the early 18th century, using slaves and prisoners, but at only a metre in height, they failed to protect the city. Now, the height had been increased to ten metres. Clinton was not impressed. "These won't last," he said loudly to the distress of our guide. The levees had a history of poor maintenance and when Hurricane Katrina hit in 2005, long after our time, they crumbled like bread crumbs. The French Quarter and the university campus escaped since they occupied higher ground. Once the capital of French Louisiana, New Orleans was a melting pot of races and cultures. Creoles, Spanish, African, French, and Acadians from Canada who had migrated south and lived in the bayous. Known as Cajuns and French in origin, they spoke an archaic dialect that few understood.

We felt strangely foreign. We were no longer part of the colonial family. Sharing a common language didn't mean a shared culture. My first social experience was unpleasant. I had been set up on a blind date. The car that turned up to collect me was a battered old Chevy. The driver and his friend seemed rather immature and had brought their own booze. Louisiana had a strict drinking policy, with no alcohol served to those under twenty-one. The girl looked vacuous. Her hair was so teased it scratched the roof.

"You know," she said, turning to me, "General Sherman took our horses."

I was confused. Wasn't it some time since the Civil War? Was there something I didn't know?

"We lost our plantation, we lost everything."

She didn't look like someone who owned a plantation; she didn't look like Scarlett O'Hara. We parked and the men started to drink. The girl and her man started to neck. I felt a hand creep up my thigh. I moved as close to the window and as far away as I could.

"Drive down to the river," ordered my date.

We drove out along the freeway, swerving across the lanes. I was terrified and grabbed hold of him.

"Faster," he shouted. "She's getting warm."

He passed the bottle around. Then we drove into the port area on the Mississippi river where the paddle steamers moored.

"There's plenty of n*****s here."

He rolled down the window and leant out shouting, "N*****s, n*****s, fucking n*****s." His voice carried on the humid air. I was beyond shock. We didn't do this sort of thing in Kenya. This guy, could he lynch people? I had read Harper Lee's *To Kill a Mockingbird*. The other two joined in with a chorus of expletives. I wanted to get back to the apartment. I did eventually get home in one piece.

In September I registered for my sophomore year. Tulane was a private liberal arts college for white students (this changed in 1963). There were no students like my blind dates. A large social divide existed between college students and those who got no further than high school. Tulane was founded in 1834 as a public medical college in response to the local epidemics of smallpox, yellow fever and cholera. The only time it closed down was during the Civil War. It is still well known for its research. It was unusual in that it had a partner college for women on its campus, which was founded by a mother in memory of her daughter. Sophie Newcomb was my alma mater, although I didn't board there since my parents lived nearby. Lessons were combined with Tulane students and degrees were awarded by Tulane. I used to walk to lessons, strolling along Charles Street lined with oak trees festooned with tresses of Spanish moss. On a track in the middle rolled the streetcar on which Tennessee Williams based his play *A Streetcar Named Desire*.

The first thing freshers did after registering was to get elected to a sorority. (The boys had their fraternities.) You had to be invited. The sororities all had Greek names. Gossip had it that there were three levels of sorority – the top was for the prettiest, cleverest and best-connected girls. I went to the 'rushes' to be vetted at tea parties where I was questioned by articulate girls with perfect hair and perfect figures. I tried several, obviously not the Jewish one since I wasn't Jewish. One asked me whether I was a Christian. "I've been confirmed," I said. It didn't convince them. Another asked about my grades. A third – which seemed rather snooty and probably in the top level – asked me whether there were any titles in my family. Well, there was Grandfather Philip. He might count and a double-barrel always sounded good. And then there was Patrick, also a Knight of the Realm. I felt sure the sorority wanted nothing less than a duke and anyway, if they only wanted me for family titles, did I want them? It was much easier choosing subjects. The system was more versatile than in Britain. You chose your main degree subject – your major – and something compatible as your minor. Then you could choose anything you liked from a huge range of modules. It was like being presented with a menu in a smart restaurant. So many choices it was difficult to decide. I chose history of Eastern art and anthropology, with French and Spanish as my mains. I had to learn Spanish from scratch but as we were close to Mexico, it seemed the obvious language to learn. And then there was something called 'Hygiene', which included tips on... hygiene and how not to get pregnant. Despite studying this module, some girls didn't manage to avoid pregnancy. One student had a backstreet abortion and bled to death. She was nineteen. Instead of hygiene, the college offered me a year's course in swimming and lifesaving. This was a useful skill and later I earned good money teaching middle-aged women how to swim. I joined one or two clubs and wrote articles for my college newspaper, *The Tulane Hullabaloo*. I had met the editor, who asked for an article on Kenya, and we went from there. The editor ended up in Vietnam. Unlike wealthier students, he failed to avoid the draft by becoming a long-term post grad.

We found somewhere decent to rent, settling on an unfurnished duplex in a wooden house in a tree-lined street near the park, which had previously been a sugar cane plantation. In 1794, a local man, Mr Étienne de Boré, planted cane brought from Cuba to replace other varieties, which had failed. The Cuban cane made Mr Boré a millionaire. Our apartment was accessed by an outside staircase. The elderly owner lived downstairs. It was in a good area and I could walk to college. We rushed out to buy furniture. It was the first time we had ever bought our own furniture and we went mad, even buying a hideous cocktail bar. On the day we moved in, as we climbed up the stairs, carrying our 'stuff', Clinton collapsed on the steps. "It's malaria," he gasped. Joan and I were unsympathetic. Clinton hadn't been near Kenya for some time and malaria had been eliminated in America by the early 1950s. "Some types of malaria can take months to develop," he insisted. He was shaking, but we weren't convinced and left him sweating on the stairs. It was indeed malaria, a rare form of it. Excited medics from Tulane rushed up and down the wooden staircase to take Clinton's blood. He became the celebrity of the medical school.

Many New Orleans inhabitants boasted French ancestry. Many were Catholics. Something of the antebellum period still lingered. There were copies of plantation homes including a Tara from *Gone with the Wind* on Charles Street where the streetcar travelled into town. I lived at home for the first time since I was twelve. I survived without a sorority. In retrospect, this was a mistake. Sorority life was fun. I might have made more local friends and it was, after all, part of American life. Besides, girls from the sororities had perks like being chosen as homecoming queen at the annual homecoming football match at the Sugar Bowl. This was the high point of the football season, when Tulane alumni returned for a weekend of parties and dances. Tulane's team, the Tulane Green Wave, played in a sub-division of the American Football Bowl. The players looked like Superman in their smart green trousers and tops with their exaggerated shoulder pads. I envied the cheerleaders in their whirly green skirts and matching pom poms. Drinking under the age of twenty-one was illegal, so students would hide bottles of vodka in their pockets.

Instead of a sorority, I made friends with students from South and Central America, Argentina, Mexico, and Colombia, and with northerners, who were considered foreign. The New Orleans girls seemed a bit cliquey but local families made up for it by hosting foreign students in their beautiful homes and gardens. We were taken through the bayous on yachts and given the run of their swimming pools. You could tell who the top families were – their girls ended up as carnival queens at Mardi Gras. They were all petite and beautiful, looked expensive and usually had good grades. (Many were Tulane girls.) It was an honour to be elected queen of a club, known as a krewe. The girls had to be unmarried and aged between eighteen and twenty-one. The krewes had names like Endymion, Bacchus or Comus. They had their own club floats on which they paraded, tossing favours into the crowd, beads, fake gold dubloons and plastic skeletons. In the evening they hosted grand balls accessible only by invitation. Every year they elected a new king. We were invited to the Ball of Proteus and ordered to appear at '9 of the clock' when a dazzlingly gold king and queen processed around the hall in their matching crowns while we all sang 'If Ever I Cease to Love'. This was first sung for the Grand Duke Alexis of Russia, who visited New Orleans in 1872. The first verse mentions the illustrious guest.

"If ever I cease to love – if ever I cease to love –
May the Grand Duke Alexis ride a buffalo through Texas
If ever I cease to love – if ever I cease to love."

There were more similar verses but this one was for him. Mardi

Gras brought crowds in from all over the world, filling the streets with revellers, bands, food and fancy dresses, secret societies and beautiful girls.

Music and food played a large part in the city's culture. There was a New Orleans Symphony Orchestra and there were the jazz clubs. New Orleans is considered the birthplace of jazz, which originated from brass band music at funerals, whereas 'The Blues' developed from the songs of the cotton and cane workers in Mississippi. A fusion of the two styles led to New Orleans jazz, with its own particular style and rhythms. And then there was the food, the product of the city's diverse heritage. Jambalayas, red beans and rice, shrimp gumbo, seafood and po' boys, huge sandwiches of crusty bread so big you struggled to fit them into your mouth. For birthday treats, we went to Brenans, or Antoines, famous for their oysters. We often strolled through the French Quarter listening to the music escaping from the open doors of the bars and cafes lining the street. One jazz bar had a famous pianist called Sweet Lil, who looked about a hundred and had lost most of her teeth. Her strong brown hands hammered the keyboard like a young girl's, improvising as she went along. Most evenings in the bars finished with the crowd singing 'Dixie' (Dixie is the nickname for the Southern US). The song originated from the minstrel shows in the 19th century and was a favourite of Abraham Lincoln's. Everyone sang loudly, they were proud southerners. I sang the song, overcome by feelings of patriotism. It had a better tune than 'God Save the Queen', but it wasn't even my history, and even though it was a rallying cry for the South, I still sang it with conviction. The first verse went like this:

> *"I wish I was in Dixie.*
> *Hooray! Hooray!*
> *In Dixie's land, I'll take my stand to live and die in Dixie.*
> *Away, away, away down south in Dixie.*
> *Away, away, away, down south in Dixie."*

New Orleans was a most agreeable city except during the hot summer holidays when the humidity levels rose and it was a struggle even to move outside. Everyone tried to get away.

Our first summer was testing. We were still finding our feet. So the suggestion from a classmate to spend the holidays in a summer camp came just in time. Summer camps were an important part of American life.

Rockbrook Camp was in the Blue Ridge Mountains of North Carolina, part of the larger Appalachian range. And they were blue, ridge upon ridge blending like an artist's colour wash. This hue is produced by the trees releasing a compound called isoprene to protect their leaves from heat stress. Our camp consisted of log huts dotted in the woods with a dining hall and kitchen by a spring-fed lake where we swam every day. The climate was kind, there were no mosquitoes, no energy-sapping humidity. The estate belonged to the daughter of the Barnum's Circus family who had eloped with the

The swimming lake at Rockbrook Camp

chauffeur. Both her sons had been killed in the Second World War and were commemorated on a rock altar in our open-air chapel. Above the camp, reached by a steep climb, were rock platforms where we would sit with our legs dangling over the edge. The meadows behind were rich with wild berries, which we picked for fruit cobblers. I was a camp counsellor, a teacher-guide who looked after the girls in my care. I taught a mixture of subjects, such as swimming, riding, hiking or crafts. We all looked like Russian Young Pioneers in our uniform of white shorts and tops with red neckties. Otherwise we wore baggy dungarees with our hair in bunches. My cabin had ten teenage girls (the camp took girls as young as eight). Savy teenagers, daughters of rich East Coasters who had been sent away for the summer, they would play all sorts of tricks like putting bowls of water on the cabin door, which fell on my head when I came to bed. There were enough risks outside such as snakes without the threat of a soaking. The most dangerous snake was the coral snake. There was a rhyme we all knew: "red on yellow, kill a fellow; red on black, venom lack."

The snakes would come out at night (shoes had to be worn), which made it hard to see which snake you trod on. Luckily the coral snake was rare and we were unlikely to encounter it.

Life in camp was idyllic. The area was glorious for walking, it was full of old Indian trails. A local man guided us and showed us how to make cups out of leaves to drink the clear stream water. In the evenings as we sat around our camp fire eating Hershey bars sandwiched together with crackers and melted marshmallows, he told us old Cherokee legends. The Cherokees were a large and sophisticated tribe who lived in the Appalachians. They were settled people who were highly organized politically and socially and well integrated with the Europeans. Like them, they had acquired black slaves. Many Indian tribes kept slaves but the wealthy Cherokee had the most. All the slave-owing tribes sided with the Confederacy during the American Civil War. Cherokee history is a complicated narrative, like most of history. Their chief, John Ross, was more Scottish than Cherokee but since his Indian heritage came through the maternal line, he was considered a full member of his tribe, and as an educated wealthy trader he was perfectly suited to plead with Washington for his people. At first the tribal lands were protected by treaties. But with the encroachment of settlers and the discovery of gold, these came under pressure. In 1830 President Andrew Jackson ignored the treaties and signed the Indian Removal Act, which granted lands west of the Mississippi to the Appalachian tribes in exchange for their ancestral land. That these lands were already home to other tribes didn't seem to matter. The act was sanctioned by Congress. Although some members of Ross's tribal council were prepared to accept financial inducements and migrate west, Ross refused. It took 7,000 armed troops to evict the Cherokee. In 1860, a year before the Civil War, 16,000 of them marched with their 2,000 slaves to Oklahoma, a journey of three months. Among the 4,000 who died was Ross's wife. In Oklahoma the Cherokee had to adapt to a different environment of open prairie and a continental climate. This migration became known as the Trail of Tears and is a national trail today. Every summer a theatrical re-enactment also called 'The Trail of Tears' took place in Ashville. The whole camp went. It was an emotional experience. Rockbrook's lands had been Cherokee lands. We were only passing through.

One week, two of us counsellors were sent on a two-day expedition to remote woods, two hours distant. We were both nineteen, in charge of ten girls aged ten to fifteen. We didn't know the area. We had no maps, no compass. We had no first aid. There was no risk assessment, no mobile phones, and we were driven there by the only man in camp, the truck driver. It was raining as the driver unloaded our tents and left. Our first duty was to erect the tents but none of us really knew how to do it and we forgot that drainage was essential, especially as it was raining. The tents flooded and as we desperately dug channels to release the flooding, we didn't

Camp counsellors with their charges – author top row second right

see the man who appeared from the trees. It was beginning to get dark. The girls fell silent.

"A hillbilly," whispered my fellow counsellor, who noticed him first.

We were terrified (and this was before the film *Deliverance*). Hillbillies were thought of as violent, backward people.

The man walked over and examined our efforts. He had blue eyes in a wrinkled face. There were red tones in his unruly beard.

"Thou ain't done it properly."

His accent was strange. He obviously didn't think much of us. We stood in the rain dripping off the trees. He put his hand in his trousers and produced a key. He led us to a cabin and opened the door. Inside were bunk beds with goose-down quilts.

"Hunting lodge. They dun give me the keys."

We all rushed in. He stoked up the wood burner then disappeared as quickly as he had arrived. We stripped down, tried to dry our clothes and opened our food supplies. An hour later he returned with a guitar, food, and eight of his eleven children. They all piled into the cabin with their ukuleles and mouth organs and gave us two hours of rollicking gospel songs.

In the morning the sun was shining. As we were putting on our boots, the door opened. We could just see the revolvers, one on each hip. Now and then our new friend drew the guns and shot into the air.

"To frighten the rattlers."

He led the way, walking lopsidedly like a cowboy, pistols at the ready. (And yes, we heard rattlers but never saw them.) We ended up at his farm, a wooden shack on stilts. There were hens, goats, pigs, a cow, a vegetable garden, a liquor still and a heavily pregnant wife. When the truck returned two days later, our new friend seemed sad to see us go.

"What kind of accent is that?" he asked me.

"English."

"That ain't no English I ever heard."

We had gone back in time. How might our adventure have ended without him? America was a place where you could have these kind of adventures, where there was so much space you could live off-grid. Our hillbilly didn't quite live off-grid. His children went to school and they all went to church. America was full of tribes of free-range citizens who seemed to exist on the periphery. Hillbillies were scattered throughout the Ozarks and the Appalachians. Most were descendants of settlers from England, lowland Scotland and Ulster. Some became coal miners, others farmers. All were poor but fiercely independent. We went back to Rockbrook in the autumn when the hills glowed red and gold. The buildings looked forlorn with no children, no one swimming in the icy lake, the truck rusting outside the main lodge. We walked back up to our rock ledges to admire the view before the winter set in and remind ourselves of its glorious emptiness. I thought of the Cherokees exiled from their homes standing on these very same ledges before they were force-marched west. This was their home. They had lived there for centuries. I felt their loss keenly. But how could I really understand? I had no lands to leave. I was a nomad, an advantage perhaps in a changing world, but unsettling nevertheless. For the Cherokee there was nowhere else to go, no pink parts of the world where, even though they didn't belong, they might have found a home.

In my second year I did what many students did. I took a job. Mine was with Gulf Oil in town. I was given a microscope and left to look at samples at different depths from the drillings to see what, if any, fossils were there. (I was studying geology at college as my science subject.) I would remove any fossils and mount them on slides, noting the well number and the depth of the drilling. This helped the geologists plot where oil might lie. I worked two days a week from 7.30 in the morning to 4pm, with a very short break for lunch. I was the only college girl working there and I earned good money. It was tiring work, sitting hunched over a microscope, concentrating on tiny fossils buried in silt. I thought of my great-grandfather Patrick Manson spending his nights in the same way, searching for even smaller parasites. It was quite usual for students to work to pay their college fees and it was easy to find such work. I had a friend called Virgil who spent his summers working in a remote soap factory in Alaska, which covered most of his fees, whereas I was working for pocket money.

Clinton said little about his work. He had a generous research budget from the American navy but he wasn't allowed to prescribe drugs without an American medical degree. It was somewhat demeaning, coming from a family who were 'tropical medicine'. Although he enjoyed fishing excursions to the Gulf, New Orleans wasn't really his sort of place but he hadn't wanted to return to England and this had been a good offer. His escapes were trips back to Kenya (financed by the American navy) where he met up with Justice, his assistant, and recreated those days on safari. He also had trips to Mexico, Brazil and Colombia where Tulane had an offshoot of its medical school. These were all countries where leishmaniasis was prevalent. Leprosy too still existed, even in America. Clinton's work included regular visits to the local leper hospital. Carville was the only in-patient hospital in continental America (there was one in Hawaii) for the treatment of leprosy. The hospital was started in 1894 when five men and two women were taken by barge to an old, abandoned sugar plant in a place called Indian Camp on a bend on the Mississippi river. Lepers were removed from their families, forcibly quarantined and treated. They never got out. One patient described it as like a monastery cut off from the world, where everyone helped each other. Feared for years, now we know that leprosy is a bacterial infection that can be treated. If left untreated, the damage to nerves in the skin, nose and eyes can never be reversed.

There had been other quarantine centres on the shores of Louisiana and Mississippi. We saw the ruins of a yellow fever quarantine station on a trip to Ship Island, one of six barrier islands in the Gulf of Mexico. The islands, all uninhabited, are the tips of a sandbar that runs the length of the Mississippi Sound. They are vulnerable to storm surges and are shrinking. We took a boat from Biloxi in Mississippi to Ship Island, the largest at seven miles long. The weather was fine, there was little wind, the beaches with their quartz-like sand were inviting. We didn't realize that there were no trees, no fresh water or that the marshes and brackish pools in the middle of the island were breeding grounds for mosquitoes. What we did know was that the boat wouldn't return until the next afternoon, so there was no going back. We were six students with one tent, some food and an over-rated sense of adventure. We were alone. We saw no animals, no migratory birds, no raccoons, feral pigs or sea turtles. Apart from the quarantine station, which had been busy in the 19th century, the only other signs of human activity were an abandoned fort and a lighthouse. In 1853 a major epidemic of yellow fever in New Orleans spread to Mississippi.

Not until 1901 did an American doctor discover that a mosquito transmitted the disease or that it was a virus and not a parasite. The symptoms are nausea, fever, muscle pain and jaundice, which turns the eyes and skin of its sufferers yellow. Many died in the epidemics. We didn't know all this and we were eaten alive. Our only escape was to sit on the jetty where the breeze discouraged insects and watch the dolphins churning up the phosphorescence in the water below. When the boat returned the next day they found us waiting on the quay, sunburnt, covered in bites and desperate for a meal.

The south, Louisiana and Mississippi and other states were clinging to the past even in the 1960s. Were it not for legislation, we felt that slavery might still exist. African Americans were second-class citizens. There was no legal apartheid like in South Africa but there remained unspoken rules. The schools and universities remained segregated until 1963. All our information on sleazy local politics came from Beth, our maid who was African American. From Beth we learnt that the white politicians who shouted the loudest and didn't back the civil rights movement were the ones who had coloured mistresses. It mattered how many white genes you had. Historically there were differing degrees of whiteness. The fairer your skin, the better you fared. I wasn't aware of, nor did I join in, any protests on campus as I lived at home. The only protest I nearly joined was a march to the African American college Dillard to support protesters there. It was the only time I fell out badly with Joan.

"When in Rome." It was her mantra.

"I'm in America."

As it turned out the protest was cancelled.

My own experience of racism, my first and last, was somewhat unusual. I was a member of a walking group. We were a diverse lot: American, Arab, Haitian, South American, all students like me. Sometimes we walked in rural Mississippi where you could find fossil remains in the dried-up tributaries of the river. It was thirsty work. When we spied a cabin in the middle of a field called 'The Black Cat Café', ice-cold cokes beckoned. I ran across the grass and pushed open the door. Twenty pairs of black eyes swivelled to stare at me. The air smelt hostile. Still, I might as well ask. After all, they would know from my accent that I wasn't a southerner.

"Ten Coca-Colas, please," I said in my best English voice, taking my dollars out of my purse.

The bar man spat his cigarette butt across the wooden floor.

"We don't serve whites here."

I slipped down the steps in my hurry to escape.

People commented on the poverty of Africa but rural Mississippi in the 1960s seemed almost as bad. We saw small subsistence farms with a pig, a cow, a goat and vegetable gardens where hens scratched at the dry soil. And yet it was fertile land – as the exploitation of cotton proved. Old men, both white and black, rocked in chairs on their porches. Where the money showed was in the beautiful plantation homes. Some had fallen into disrepair but were still elegant in their decay. Others were lived in. Some were enormous like the palaces in St Petersburg, others more like French farmhouses. One of the most beautiful was Oak Alley in rural Louisiana, which was approached by its avenue of arching oak trees, their trunks mottled with green moss. Oak Alley was built by slaves with bricks made on site. It started as a pecan farm but became a 'white gold' plantation, as sugar cane was called. Oak Alley survived the Civil War, its economy destroyed but with the house still standing. Now it rents out cottages and does bed and breakfast for the tourists.

Sugar became a major crop during the 1820s and 30s. It offered greater profits than cotton but with greater risks and it required armies of slaves and expensive machinery. The physical demands were so great that no slave lived to old age. Some slave owners were not what you might expect. Marie-Thèreze Métoyer, known by her African name Coincoin, created a plantation with her fourteen children and her own slaves on a plot of land left to her by her white husband. She was not the only ex-slave to prosper in this way.

When we were in New Orleans, the Ku Klux Klan had reassembled to oppose the civil rights movement. There was little trouble in New Orleans, but out in Georgia, Alabama and Mississippi, Klan members were running around in white robes brandishing burning crosses, setting churches on fire and murdering people both black and white. They hated most the white supporters of civil rights and they hated John F Kennedy. It was later that year, on the 22nd of November, that President Kennedy was assassinated. Like the Twin Towers it seemed as if a line had been drawn before Kennedy and after Kennedy. It marked a watershed in all our lives. I had just finished lessons and was walking across campus clutching my books when I saw students running around like ants whose nest had been destroyed. People crowded around cars, listening to radios. Words escaped: shot, Kennedy. Some girls openly wept. Even the oak trees seemed to droop with the news, their moss braids limp like widows' hair. I ran home hoping he was still alive. Joan was crying in the kitchen. She had been to the supermarket when Kennedy's death was announced over the tannoy. She usually returned complaining about women shopping in their curlers. The white customers had cheered while the black customers wept. We saw Jack Ruby shot live on television. Only two years previously we had lived through the Cuban Missile Crisis, following the Soviet Union's building of nuclear missile sites on Cuba, only ninety miles from US shores. Every day we feared a nuclear war. After thirteen days of negotiation, the missiles were removed. (We didn't know then that a deal was made between the two powers: Soviet missiles out of Cuba in return for American nuclear missiles out of Italy and Turkey.) And now, the man who had negotiated this deal had been assassinated. It seemed like the end of an era but it wasn't. It was a beginning, with the Civil Rights Act of 1964 tightened up in 1965 under President Lyndon Johnson.

In the summer of '64, before my final year, my Spanish professor suggested going to summer school in Mexico. All I knew of Mexico came from westerns, which showed Mexicans tramping through deserts in their sombreros. Clinton had another useful friend, a Mexican doctor who would meet me at the airport. I took a flight south.

Pablo Neruda, the great Chilean poet, called Mexico "the last of the magic countries". Like a piñata, it released its magic to those who sought it. The piñata is a symbol of the two cultures of Mexico. It was brought to Mexico by the Spaniards but a similar tradition existed for the Aztec god Huitzilopochtli's birthday in December, the Aztec month of the Descent of Water.

My first shock was that no one met me at the airport. A voice over the tannoy called out my name. Clinton's friend had suffered a family tragedy. I had to find a hotel. Outside the airport the territory was threatening for a 'gringa' – all Western girls were called 'gringas', although the term usually meant American and easy prey. I had been warned of taxis that would cart you off, steal everything and throw you out onto the highway or worse. The offers continued at the desk of the hotel, from the waiter who delivered a meal to my room. It was no better in the morning as I waited for the bus to the university. Men fought to pay my fare. I was tempted to take a pesero – a shared taxi that crossed the city daily – but my Spanish was weak and how would I know which was the right pesero? I didn't relax until I had crossed into the Campus of UNAM, the National University of Mexico, forcing my way through the hordes of hustlers whose grandmothers, mothers and aunts offered cheap accommodation. In front of me towered the rectangular Central Library, ten storeys high, its walls covered in murals. From where I stood one stared back at me with the face of an Aztec god. Above the entrance was written: "*For my people, the spirit shall speak*". It sounded like a line from an Aztec poem.

It was exciting to be part of this modern campus, the largest in Latin America, highly ranked for its research, and now a UNESCO World Heritage Site. I found accommodation too. My landlady was no fake grandmother. She was a respectable professor at the university. Angela (Chela) Martinez del Rio lived in Colima Street in the city in a three-storey town house with a grand gate and large windows. She came from an important colonial family who had lost their homes and land during the Mexican Revolution in 1910, which was followed by a decade of bloodshed. One minute relaxing on your hacienda, the next hanging from a tree. Mexico had had so many revolutions and presidents, it was hard to keep count. Chela was a child during that dark decade and remembered much of it. Now she reigned over our house like a matriarch. There were several of us, three maids, four students, three Mexican ladies in their forties and Chela who looked like a newly born bird, all bones, no feathers, gasping for breath. She was badly asthmatic and suffered from the pollution that hung over the city in a menacing cloud.

Chela's house was a proper family home with heavy colonial furniture, family portraits, shaded rooms and a tiled patio like a Roman atrium. My bedroom on the second floor had previously been a dining room. It had internal sliding glass doors and no window. Gloomy oil paintings hung on the wall. One night an earthquake struck and the large painting above my bed crashed onto the floor. The house swayed horribly. I ran upstairs to join the maids, who clutched their crucifixes and prayed loudly. The safest place is always underneath the staircase on the ground floor but I was terrified of dying alone. The tremors lasted barely a minute but it seemed like hours.

Every day after classes, we returned to Colima for a formal lunch at a table laid with china and silver. Light supper served at 10pm was usually a bowl of chocolate made from cacao pods pounded to a thick paste by the maids in the kitchen. Like the Aztec drink, it was flavoured with vanilla or honey, never with sugar.

Lunch at Chela's house in Mexico City

We were a household of women like in Lorca's play *The House of Bernarda Alba*, protected by grills on the windows and gates that were locked at midnight. I acquired a boyfriend, a medical student – I didn't have to whisper to him through bars on the windows. I received letters delivered on a silver salver by a maid. Ricardo was on Chela's approved list, so I could go out with him. As long as we were back before the gates closed, it didn't matter where we went, although Chela preferred us to go to art exhibitions instead of a drinking dive on a volcanic ridge overlooking the city where no respectable Mexican girl would ever be seen. We were also taken to private parties where the Mexican girls huddled like wallflowers around the edge of the room while we gringas were much sought after, for what we promised, not for what we looked like. If looks could kill, we'd all have died on the spot. The girls got their men in the end.

Like most of the Mexican upper classes, Ricardo looked more European than indigenous (although they all boasted of royal

Aztec blood). The faces we saw in the street were more properly indigenous. These were the winners who had survived war, disease and slavery. Their genes showed in their short stocky bodies, their dark skin, their narrow eyes and their long, heavy plaits. But they were still poor, remarkably cheerful and with a huge capacity for enjoyment. In 1965 the population of Mexico City was just over six million. Now, the population of greater Mexico City is more like twenty-six million. In 2006 the city was judged to have the largest slum in the world, known rather quaintly as a 'lost city'. There were slums in the 60s but they were smaller and on the edge of the city, so we didn't see this side. We were drawn into the heart of the city, the centre too of its Aztec predecessor. One sky scraper dominated, the forty-four-storey Torre Latinoamericana, a monochrome building layered with bands of windows that looked like rulers. It was drab and out of place among the colonial mansions and the lopsided baroque cathedral. This was a city that exploded with colour. The cubist houses painted pink, orange, turmeric and cobalt blue seemed to grow organically out of the earth. In the lava flow of Pedregal, houses were built over volcanic boulders, which merged into the rooms like furniture. It was ultra modern and yet it was ancient. Everywhere, the city reminded me of what had gone before. Aztec temples, the tall ahuehuete trees in the park which dated from Montezuma's time and were known as the Montezuma bald cypress. There was the tree under which Cortes wept after his defeat on the Noche Triste. In the main square performers dressed like Aztec warriors, eagle or leopard, feathers or fur, beak or head, and danced on the uneven cobbles. At the Basilica of Guadalupe the devout crawled on their bleeding knees for redemption as did their equally devout ancestors running with flares across the mountains. The Catholic church knew how to channel this magic and create a mixture of the fantastic and the mythical. In the Floating Gardens of Xochimilco you could see what was left of the Aztec islands where much of their food was grown. Sturdy Aztec-looking matrons paddled past with the mariachi bands that accompanied them. It was here on a boat where I had the label 'Gringa' screamed at me, and not in admiration.

While I was in Mexico City, the new Museum of Anthropology had just been built in the style of an Aztec palace. Statues were being moved there from all over the country. When the statue of Tlaloc the Rain God was lifted in to its new site it poured for days without the need for a child sacrifice. I felt sorry for Montezuma, who lost everything. Later I wrote a novel about him. But from this merging of cultures and religions evolved unique styles of art and architecture created by indigenous workmen. Diego Rivera, the most famous of the Mexican muralists, was partially indigenous and painted history as he saw it. For me his most appealing work was in the old Jesuit chapel of Mexico's School of Agricultural Studies at Chapingo. I had taken a local bus, which was full of peasants with their sacks of corn, chickens and pigs. A drunken man got on clutching a bottle of milky fluid from which he sipped noisily. He saw me and held the bottle in front of my face. I saw the cactus fibres swimming in the liquid and the froth and spittle like a murky Milk of Magnesia. I choked. He was offended by my refusal. Fortunately I got off the bus before him. Above the entrance to the school was written:

"To teach the exploitation of the land and not of men."

The chapel, sometimes referred to as the Sistine Chapel of Mexico, tells the story of the creation in Mexican style. It was like no art I had ever seen. There were none of the fields and cows of English art or portraits of the country squires who owned them. This was political with no religious images. Painted in niches are the shrouded bodies of the buried martyrs whose blood fertilizes the soil. Porthole windows are framed with red petals like flares radiating from the sun. In the apse a naked Virgin Earth holds the seed corn in her hand while beneath her, men work the machinery of industrialization. The colours were the rich tones of the earth and the brown bodies of the people who inhabited it.

Sometimes our lectures at university ended up in heated discussions – many of our tutors were refugees from the Spanish Civil War. One had been a member of Garcia Lorca's tertulia. He would jump to his feet during lectures. "I will never return to Spain until Franco is dead!" We all shouted, "Death to Franco!" Coming from such a conservative family, life-long readers of *The Daily Telegraph*, I found this heady stuff. There were so many students at UNAM that classes were held in shifts. The Medical School was the most crowded, with classes that lasted into the night. My language and literature classes included modules in colonial and indigenous literature. The Aztec language (Nahuatl) was musical, full of metaphors and well suited to poetry. Poems could be heroic sagas or reflections on the impermanence of life.

Oh friends this earth is only lent to us,
We shall have to leave our fine poems,
We shall have to leave our beautiful flowers.
That is why I am sad as I sing for the sun.

The Aztec culture was still there if you looked for it.

In theory Mexico was a democracy and elections were held, but in reality there was only one party and it couldn't be defeated. This only changed after 1968. In 1968, during the Olympic year, matters came to a head. The military occupied the university campus. Ten days before the games, 10,000 students packed into the Plaza de las Tres Culturas surrounding the remains of the Pyramid of Tlatelolco, one of three cities in the Aztec alliance. It was here in 1521 that the city finally fell to the Spanish after a long, drawn-out siege. An inscription in the plaza reads:

"This was neither victory nor defeat,
It was the sad birth of the Mestizo people
Which is Mexico today."

Now the students gathered for their own battle. Armoured vehicles
and soldiers surrounded the square. The shooting began after 6pm.
No one is sure how many students and workers were killed. But the
government action was shocking and something changed. Like the
brutal battles of 1521, it was both an end and a beginning. There had
been other battles, too, with the closest neighbour, the United States,
who seized the states of California, Arizona, Colorado, Nevada,
Utah and Texas from Mexico in 1848. There is a saying:

"Poor Mexico, so far from God and so close to the United
States."
Now the wars are drug wars.

I made a new friend. Carmen lived in Texas and had been sent
south to summer school. She was bi-lingual and had dual American
and Mexican citizenship. We sat together in literature classes. She
called me Isabelita. The Mexicans love diminutives and I loved them
too.
"How about being a queen for a day?"
"Queen?"
"Queen of the bullfight. There will be nine of us. We dress up in
regional costumes and parade around the bull ring in cars. We'll be
on television."
It sounded good. First I had to acquire a costume. Mine was
an Adelita, the garish dress of a camp follower during the 1910
revolution. It was pink and lime-green satin with lashings of black
lace. I had a black shawl and carried a bouquet of red carnations,
with a matching spray behind one ear. Our escort, Rancho Aguilar, a
louche cowboy, sheltered under a sombrero, large enough to fend off

a hurricane. All you could see of his face was the cigarette dangling from his lips. He wore a low-slung belt on his low-slung hips. The spurs on his boots clanked impressively when he moved. We felt like Hollywood stars as we rode around the bull ring in Cadillacs to the roars of the crowd, ending up in the 'royal' box from where we watched the bloody proceedings. Some evenings we went to Garibaldi Square, where the mariachis congregated. Once a troupe of them turned up at Colima Street and serenaded a fellow lodger whose birthday it was. They looked magnificent in their silver-braided sombreros, their black and silver shirts and trousers and their buckled belts. But it was a tenuous way to make a living. They probably came from those slums we didn't know existed.

In September Clinton drove down from New Orleans to give a series of lectures at the Medical School. They paid him with a gold fifty-peso coin with the Aztec emblem of an eagle and a serpent sitting on a cactus. It was mouth-wateringly heavy and made of solid gold. After his lectures, Clinton joined an expedition in Western Mexico with some Mexican doctors and parasitologists. We drove to Oxaca where we would wait for him to emerge from the back country. After a week a message came via bush telegraph that "the big señor with the bald head" was ready for collection. Off we set. It was a long journey on terrible tracks. Finally after hours of travelling deeper and deeper into the interior and climbing endless sierras in Zapotec country, we reached a sandy clearing in a forest with a cluster of houses. One or two men sat outside in the street. Young boys came to look us over. Even here, in this poor hamlet, the church dominated the village. People started coming back from the fields and wanted to chat. My pukka university Spanish wasn't up to the task. They all knew about the 'big señor with the bald head'. They giggled and pointed to the hills. We sweated in the heat. Some hours later, as the sun was fading, Clinton strode out of the forest, grinning boyishly. We drove away to Acapulco, where we stayed in the cheap end of town. Clinton saved money by boiling the breakfast eggs in a plug-in egg boiler on top of the lavatory cistern. Joan and I sat on the beach drinking cokes and staring at the Pacific. It wasn't long before a handsome youth sat down next to us, making a beeline for Joan. "Why did he bother with an old lady like me?" asked Joan when he left. Even I, naïve as I was, could recognize a gigolo when I saw one.

After our week, we drove north to the Texan border, over the bridge on the Rio Grande, where the Mexican Customs stopped us and asked whether we had any gold coins. It was apparently against the law to take gold currency out of the country. We all glared at Clinton. "No, no, no…" we mouthed. But yes. He held out the coin. It glittered tantalizingly in the sun. The customs officials' eyes widened. Who knew where it ended up, probably not in the government coffers. We didn't speak to Clinton for the rest of the trip.

Graduation at Tulane, the author with Clinton and Joan

I got my degree in French and Spanish. But I failed to find a husband. A southern girl was expected to graduate with a good degree and a fiancé. I never forgot Mexico. I went back in 2001. It had changed. There were more people, more buildings, more litter, less water, better museums full of newly-discovered Aztec artefacts. There were more sky scrapers, more steel, and the modern architecture was dazzling. The mariachis still sang. It was still vibrant, humming with life and optimism. The magic remained but sometimes you had to search for it.

EPILOGUE

I felt ready to conquer the world. But I didn't know where to start. So I decided to return to England. Clinton was horrified. I had a green card. I could work anywhere in America. Anywhere. I didn't want anywhere. The world was full of anywheres. But I was well placed in America with a Tulane degree. I could have done a master's in Mexican studies at Tulane. Anything was possible. So why the sudden nostalgia for somewhere I had barely lived? I wanted to belong. And there was something else that concentrated my mind. During my last year I was taken on a visit to Texas by a medical student friend who had relations in a small town called Center in East Texas close to the border with Louisiana. My friend, neither partner nor lover, had been around for three years. He was a gentle, generous, civilized man. The Texan family welcomed me warmly. But I was there under false pretences. This was a family reunion. I wasn't family. I should never have agreed to go. I knew what they were thinking. The questions came, polite but probing. "Where do you go to church?" I gulped. This wasn't the place to say I didn't. I was among staunch Christians here.

"I'm Church of England."

They looked relieved. I slept that night in a quiet room full of old family furniture. On the chest opposite my bed a statue of the Buddha nodded frantically. Was he warning me? Next day I went to church.

"Do you bake cookies at your church?" asked a mousy woman. "We take it in turns to bake for the services here."

My future flashed through my mind, baking cookies for the church, helping at Sunday school. This was small-town America, a neat little place with clean streets and houses with picket fences and an uneventful life. These were kind people but they seemed remote from my world. It felt so far away from what mattered. Center was not unpleasant. It had its pine forests and the Sabine River, which snaked its way 500 miles south to the Gulf of Mexico. There were worse places to live. But here the opportunities were limited. This was not what I wanted for 'home'. What would I do? I would disappear before I could make my mark. No one would even notice I had gone.

When I left they wished me well. Had they hoped for some kind of announcement? This experience was a warning. The life on offer from my friend might be in a pleasant southern town, if not Center, then somewhere like North or South Carolina with their cities of Charlotte and Charleston. There were good universities there too but there would still be church and cookies and people who didn't believe in evolution. There were the northern cities too but I knew no one there. California seemed a bit whacky. I had an Italian friend from Rome. She was bright, beautiful and chic. Like me she had travelled the world. She ended up in a dead end of Louisiana married to a fellow college student. Clinton asked how I planned to earn my living in London. I speak and write two languages, I told him. Everyone would want to employ me. Clinton laughed. He said they would only be interested in my shorthand and typing speeds.

I decided to try London despite my parents remaining in New Orleans. I had cousins in England. Everyone asked about my speeds.

I had nowhere to live, no job. I found a hostel in Kensington run by a spiritualist. It offered a room with breakfast and dinner. I got a night shift office job working for an airline. I made no friends. I slept in the day. I thought about those big landscapes in Texas. Kenya flitted through my mind. But who would welcome me there? I thought about the Blue Ridge mountains and the Cherokees on their 'trail of tears' to Oklahoma and how they had struggled to survive. I saw the dogwood trees in bloom. I thought of Mexico and its magic. I thought too about how my ancestors had moved for work. I was the result of their success. I should fit in anywhere, shouldn't I? I agreed to take a three-month graduate typing course at Pitman's. What shocked me were the number of Oxford women graduates with first-class degrees. But Clinton was right, damn him. Once I had acquired those skills, I had some wonderful jobs. I got in with an interesting crowd. I found a flat share with four girls. They became my family.

And then one day while walking in Kensington Gardens I came across the Royal Geographical Society. Standing proud, high on the wall, were two statues. David Livingstone clutching his bible and Ernest Shackleton in his sledging clothes. I went inside the building to find the bust of one of my heroines, Freya Stark. Further along the corridor was Lady Jane Franklin, who had caused problems for my ancestor in Alexandria. In the basement were treasures, Inuit boots, leopards' claws from the Congo, Shackleton's helmet, Livingstone's cap and a part of the trunk of the Iroko tree where his heart was buried. Livingstone died of the two great killers, dysentery and malaria. Shackleton died of a heart attack. The library boasted 150,000 bound volumes and the map collection was famous. I was among friends. I asked to join and despite being no geographer I became a fellow. This was a familiar world. Here were people I could recognize, who had travelled to all corners of the globe for work. On my first visit to an evening lecture, I found myself sitting next to an elderly gent. We fell into conversation.

"My dear," he confided, "I hate to eat alone. Would you come back with me for a boiled egg?"

Over boiled eggs and toast I found out that he was a world expert on the butterflies and moths of Iran. He spoke Farsi and Arabic. He knew so much. And I thought, as I listened to him, how he carried his riches in his head. There were other fellows like my new friend, all pleased to welcome a young person into their midst. These were people like me, peripatetic, rootless, who had found their home here. Now I could travel the world and still get home to bed. The talk was of distant tribes, deserts, diseases, tropical plants and further into the polar regions. And then I discovered another curious coincidence. Selim Aga, the Sudanese slave boy rescued by my ancestor in Egypt, had walked through these very same doors seeking approval and money for an expedition to West Africa. He had written:

"It is my intention next dry season to make a hunting excursion into the interior and with a view to visit Kano and the Hausa Country I will try if possible to recover the papers and books of the late Dr. Vogel, now I believe in possession of Sidi Ali the Great Shereif of Mohammedan Africa.

With this view I write request (sic) the countenance of the Royal Geographical Society to aid my efforts in procuring a gratuity for the purchase of presents for the King and Chiefs of the Yoruba, Nufeh [?] and the Faria [?] countries, and also a suitable gift to Sidi Ali of Kano to induce him to give up those valuable papers. The journey there and back will not occupy more than five months.

I have the honour to be Your Obedient humble Servant, Selim Aga."

Some years later I returned to Kenya to bury Clinton's ashes among the guinea fowl in Samburu. The plains stretched towards a line of lazy volcanoes. The skies were enormous and flushed with stars. This was the world before man. I saw how my parents had been seduced by this country. Why didn't I feel the same? I felt like a traitor. But times had changed. The world had shrunk. I went on two safaris. One, to a private camp run by an Indian family on Maasai land (both the family and the Maasai benefitted), was like the old days, with night rides in an open-top car while a young boy crouched on the running board holding a lamp to light our path. Eyes shone in the dark; we heard nightjars and the rumbles of mammals. One afternoon I asked to go on a walk and was given a young guide and a scarred old soldier with a gun to protect me from wild creatures. Claude, my guide, spoke impeccable English and knew everything about the flora and fauna. He was passionate about the environment. His parents had been against his studies. Why couldn't he do something more useful? Yet Claude, with all his erudition and charm, had difficulty in finding a full-time job. Sadly, such hunger for education didn't always lead to work in Kenya. I went to Mombasa and saw the kind of work on offer. The beaches were crowded with tourists looking for a good time. Young African men in white suits paced the beaches offering to supply it. They were handsome and intelligent like Claude. The tourists, both men and women, were old and fat. I hoped the money was good.

And what of Clinton and Joan? They came back to London and bought a mews house in Bayswater on the District line, which shook whenever the trains rumbled past. Clinton looked at the wrought-iron staircase and wondered how his coffin would be carried out (it wasn't). The house was cosy but dark, squashed between converted garages and the railway line. Little sunlight penetrated through. Joan's daily walks were across the park to Harrods. She still talked of 'God's Own Country' and it wasn't Britain. Clinton would have preferred to live in the country but he rejoined a beagling group in Kent for whom he had been a youthful whipper-in. But Kent wasn't the same. There was more barbed wire, more roads and a different kind of landowner, who didn't want beagle packs on their land. There was less room for field sports. They settled into the mews. Their network of colonial friends had shrunk. Only one or two had returned to the 'home country'. Clinton followed in the footsteps of his father and grandfather. He became a senior lecturer at the London School of Hygiene and Tropical Medicine. He also worked as consultant physician to the Overseas Development Agency and the Commonwealth Development Corporation and did two stints for World Health in Tanzania and Burma. He shared the editorship of three editions of *Manson's Tropical Diseases*, now in its 23rd edition. Latterly he held many senior positions at the Royal Society of Tropical Medicine, eventually becoming their honorary archivist. It might be said that he lived in the shadow of his more famous father and grandfather but his legacy was no less important. In 1995, the Royal Society of Tropical Medicine and Hygiene awarded him its most prestigious medal, the Manson Medal. Clinton had assured me he wouldn't get it; he hadn't done enough original research. But the committee decided otherwise. It was, said Clinton, grinning wickedly, the one medal his father never got. It was the one medal he wanted.

Clinton was the last link in three generations of tropical medicine, a fact duly noted in his obituaries in the national papers. Especially good was the one in *The Guardian*. Clinton hated the *Guardian*, too left wing, all that liberal guilt. But they gave him a wonderful send-off. He was a life-long Tory and *Daily Telegraph* reader but they failed even to notice his passing. Joan was never the same after his death. Her memory faded. She ended up in a home in Norfolk where she told tales of old Africa. When four African nurses turned up to work at the home, she thought she had returned to the Muthaiga Club in Nairobi. She died, demented, at eighty-nine, still living in Kenya in her mind.

There is no doubt that sending us away to school damaged our relationship with our parents. My brother was only nine when he left home. During the vulnerable teenage years he felt neglected. For me the rift was less noticeable. My exile only lasted three years, compared to his eight. But there were compensations. Our parents made no demands on us. We knew how to navigate the world. We joked that we could survive anywhere with a rucksack. Like my entomologist friend, we carried our assets in our heads.

And what really grounded me for good? I got married. He was from Surbiton. What could be more settled than Surbiton?

SELECT BIBLIOGRAPHY

PATRICK MANSON, THE FATHER OF TROPICAL MEDICINE
By Sir Philip Manson-Bahr CMG, DSO, MD, FRCP
British Men of Science Series
Thomas Nelson & Sons Ltd 1962

THE LIFE AND WORK OF SIR PATRICK MANSON
By Philip H Manson-Bahr DSO, MD, FRCP,
And A Alcock CIE, LLD Aberd, FRS, LIEUT. COLONEL IMS (retired)
Cassell & Co Ltd 1927

SELIM AGA: A SLAVE'S ODYSSEY
By James McCarthy
Luath Press Ltd Edinburgh 2006

F.A.N.Y. THE STORY OF THE WOMEN'S TRANSPORT SERVICE 1907–
1984
By Hugh Popham
Leo Cooper in association with Secker & Warburg 1984

IMPERIAL MEDICINE: PATRICK MANSON AND THE CONQUEST
OF TROPICAL DISEASE
By Douglas M. Haynes
University of Pennsylvania Press 2001

PATRICK MANSON AT HOME – 21 QUEEN ANNE STREET AS A HYBRID SPACE
By Dr Kristin Hussey – winner of the McCarthy Award for the History of Medicine Research
McCarthy Award lecture given at the Royal College of Physicians Edinburgh 2018

THE MILKY WAY: THE HISTORY OF THE DAIRY FARM
By Nigel Cameron
The Dairy Farm Company Ltd Hong Kong 1986

FROM THE GREENWICH HULKS TO OLD ST PANCRAS: A HISTORY OF TROPICAL DISEASE IN LONDON
G C Cook
The Athlone Press 1992

I should like to thank 'Amoy Bill' – Dr William N Brown, Academic Director in the School of Management at Xiamen University, Fujian, China – for his wonderful blogs and collected histories on Old Amoy, which he publishes on his website amoymagic.com.

BV - #0067 - 110124 - C3 - 216/138/15 - PB - 9781805141549 - Matt Lamination